D1447241

Laughter, Tears, and In-Between

Laughter, Tears, and In-Between

Soulful Stories for the Journey

PAUL S. WILLIAMS

Judson Press
VALLEY FORGE

Laughter, Tears, and In-Between: Soulful Stories for the Journey

Bible quotations in this volume are from HOLY BIBLE: New International Version, copyright © 1973, 1978, 1984. Used by permission of Zondervan Bible Publishers.

Library of Congress Cataloging-in-Publication Data

Williams, Paul, 1948–
    Laughter, tears, and in-between : soulful stories for the journey / Paul S. Williams.
        p.   cm.
    ISBN 0-8170-1383-0 (pbk. : alk. paper)
    1. Christian life—Anecdotes 2. Williams, Paul, 1948—Anecdotes.
I. Title
    BV4517.W55   2001
    242—dc21   00-060343

Printed in Canada

07 06 05 04 03 02 01

10 9 8 7 6 5 4 3 2 1

For Cathryn, Jonathan, Jael, and Jana,
who ever so graciously walk with me on this journey

CONTENTS

Just Noticing

The Journey

PREFACE

IT SEEMS THE NEED FOR STORY IS PHYSIOLOGICAL. THINK ABOUT IT. I'm told we humans can't sleep without dreaming. And when was the last time you had a dream that wasn't in story form? Like I said, the need for story is downright physiological.

I remember Dad lying next to our beds telling stories about cowboys Jim and Jiggles to my brother and me. I never knew he was making up the stories line by line as he told them. I just lay there breathlessly, glancing every now and then at my Hopalong Cassidy watch, knowing that although it looked bleak, somehow in the next ten minutes the good guys were gonna win. A gasp from my brother would send Dad down one story line. A yawn from me and he'd yank out a subplot. To me the stories seemed well told, with characters perfectly developed in love.

Just a few years later I was lying on the floor between the beds of my own children, spinning yarns about bears that tickled children and peculiar purple creatures whose evil deeds were always transformed to good.

I speak often on camera, as well as to small audiences and large audiences around the country. I get nervous before I speak, but I settle in when I tell the first story. The stories don't illustrate my points. They are my points.

Stories seem to find their own level. Children know the dark forest where wolves lie in wait. Adults know it too. The adults may understand a little more about the subtle hues of the darkness, but the children see more vividly the eyes of the wolf. Each hears the story at a particular time and place along the route of his or her unique journey. The story is their story.

Most of the stories in this book have a point, though not all of them do. They tend to be grouped around the major themes of life—growing up, family, work, being afraid of losing oneself before ever really finding oneself. If there is a thread through most it is the thread of journey. I hope the stories of my journey resonate with your stories and your journey.

Jesus had a predisposition to speaking through stories. His story about the father who had two sons is my favorite story of all time. It's because I'm both of those sons. And I have that Father.

ACKNOWLEDGMENTS

COUNTLESS PEOPLE HAVE ENCOURAGED ME OVER THE YEARS, beginning with my parents, David and Margaret Williams. There are some whose assistance on this particular collection of stories deserves special mention, however.

I am grateful for the generous help and insight offered by Jim Phegley, David Reynolds, Dusty Rubeck, Rick Rusaw, Anne Snock, Tony Twist, and Myron Williams. Special thanks to Philip Kenneson and Randy Frame for their valuable assistance, and to my executive assistant, Brigida Kelley, for her tireless and always excellent work.

Rememberings

1

Opening the Gate for Pa

WHEN I WAS A YOUNG BOY THERE WAS NOTHING I LOVED MORE than visiting my maternal grandparents in eastern Kentucky. My grandfather operated a farm owned by a small college. He and Grandma lived in a little two-bedroom brick house across the road from the campus. There was a flower-covered front porch, a dark henhouse out back, and a summer kitchen.

On each visit I'd wake up early in the morning, but still well after Pa, as we called my grandfather, had gone to the barn to milk the cows. I'd smell Grandma's fresh biscuits and enjoy the pleasure of picturing them turning light brown in the pan. A few minutes later those still-warm biscuits would be covered with molasses or smothered with butter and jam—a five-year-old's delight.

With the smell of breakfast still lingering in the summer kitchen I'd pace in front of the screen door on the back porch and strain to hear Pa's old red Farmall tractor chugging up the path. When he arrived he'd turn off the motor, head into the kitchen, and take a long slow drink from his dipper. I imagined it was the same dipper he had used when they hadn't had running water and he had to draw his drink from deep in the water bucket. Pa would wipe his mouth with his sleeve and head

toward the tractor. His quick "Come on!" was all that was spoken, and I would follow his giant strides out the back door.
When I was precariously perched on the tractor hitch and hanging onto the back of Pa's tractor seat for dear life, we'd head
down the path behind the boys' dorm and out toward the barn.
When we got to the gate I enjoyed the highlight of my morning.

Pa would stop the tractor and I would hop off, take the clasp
off the gate, and proudly pull it open. Pa would drive the tractor
through the gate, and I'd muscle it closed, return the clasp to its
place, and hop back on the tractor hitch. Only now I had to be
at least two inches taller than when I'd gotten off the tractor. I
had opened the gate for Pa! I doubt it felt any better when Neil
Armstrong took that one giant leap for mankind.

I don't remember when Pa first taught me to remove the clasp
and push the gate open. But it was the stuff of growing up. I
could do something Pa could do. Something he taught me to do.
And I remember how marvelous it felt time and again to watch
that tractor drive through the gate I had muscled open.

Through buttered biscuits and small chores encouraged to com-
pletion, Grandma and Pa gave a tangible piece of themselves to a
five-year-old boy, to hold and remember and carry on the journey.
Concrete acts of love. Few words spoken, but memories created
that when stirred still bring a scent of biscuits frying up light
brown in the pan.

*God, you are the one with the power to march through the gates of
hell. Yet you made yourself known to a small boy through an open
farm gate and the thoughtful gaze of a loving grandfather. Thank you
for gifting us with your presence in treasured moments of joy. AMEN.*

2

The Quilters at 506 Noah Avenue

I WAS ABOUT FIVE YEARS OLD, AND IT WAS OUR TUESDAY RITUAL. MY brother was at school, and Dad picked up Mom and me in the big green Chevy. Then we drove to 506 Noah Avenue.

We generally walked in the side door. From the landing just inside the door you could go upstairs or downstairs. I was always hoping we went straight downstairs. I felt uncomfortable in the upstairs living room. It was dark, and prominently displayed against the wall was an oiled walnut console radio, about three feet tall, with ivory-looking buttons imprinted with the call letters of each regional radio station. The button to the far right was for WAKR. I knew that one because my brother listened to that station when snow caused hopes of an unscheduled vacation day from Schumacher Elementary School.

On the mantle above the big dark radio sat an ominous-looking clock. When its rich, deep chimes bonged on the quarter hour, the sound seemed a little otherworldly to my five-year-old senses. The big radio. The dark room.

I preferred when we walked through the side door and headed straight to the basement. It seemed larger than the rest of the house, though it wasn't, and for a basement it was unusually bright. The room was also a little cool and damp, like basements are supposed to be. Next to one wall was everything needed for a complete kitchen—in a basement! The wonder of that. There were cabinets, a stove, a sink, and all the pots, pans, and utensils necessary to prepare lunch for the church quilters.

Through my early grade school years I struggled to make out the words in the church bulletin. As I grew older I realized the printed announcement was always the same. "Quilters: Tuesday noon at the Winkler home, 506 Noah Avenue."

We generally arrived shortly before lunch, just as the food was brought to the giant tables in the basement and the women took a break from their needles and thread. I didn't pay much attention to the quilts. I was more interested in the meal. There were lots of women, most of whom were of retirement age.

Those wonderful women took more delight in me than I understood. I was decidedly shy and didn't appreciate having seasoned hands tousle my already tousled curly hair. But I did my duty until the fried chicken came, followed by the chocolate cream pie. And the tousled hair seemed a small price to pay for such delights.

When I was a few years older, maybe ten or so, I began to notice the quilts. I didn't attend the meals anymore. I was in school, and maybe Mom and Dad went without me. I really don't know. But I did notice that on special occasions quilts made their way to people as gifts from the church quilters. I thought they were pretty, and looked warm, and would make great tents to hang from a clothesline in the backyard.

Mom was pretty particular about her quilts from the church quilters. No quilters' quilt was going to be a tent, fastened by clothespins to a clothesline and pounded by clothespin spikes into the ground. I remember the drill. When we dared to use a good blanket, let alone a quilt, Mom would call out from the basement, "Dave, do you have any idea how this blanket got a hole in it?" "Well, I have no idea, Margaret," was Dad's standard reply. We'd lie low and try to avoid her shrewd questions. "You boys didn't use this blanket for a tent, did you?" We might take a risk with a good blanket every now and then, but we knew the quilts were off limits. We stuck with the old wool army blankets.

Mom always spoke of Mrs. Winkler as if she were the chief executive officer and chairman of one of the most important organizations north of the Ohio River. It seemed she was servant to kings, part saint, and cook of all things good. I was sure of the saint and cook part. As I grew older I began to understand the depths of her sainthood. She brought together otherwise idle hands and orchestrated quilts.

I became a teenager and forgot about the quilts. The church moved, changed its name, and no longer advertised "Quilters: Tuesday noon at the Winkler home, 506 Noah Avenue." We moved to Kentucky and I grew up, no longer afraid of chiming clocks and oiled wood radios. But the quilters kept on quilting.

I went to college, started to work, and married. When we opened our wedding gifts, there was a quilt. It said simply "From the Quilters." But those simple words didn't tell the story. The story was told in the patches, stitches, and colors and all those seasoned hands that had brought them together.

We still have the quilt. Its edges are frayed. A friend once restitched them, but other edges frayed. The quilt may be my favorite thing in the house. If another hurricane comes through and they order an evacuation of my neighborhood, I'll do the same thing I did the last time. I'll take the quilt to the highest level of the house and put it deep inside the cedar chest—and remember Mrs. Winkler and the quilters at 506 Noah Avenue.

God, our nurturer and provider, through patchwork quilts sewn by loving hands you warm us with your presence. AMEN.

3

When Is It
Time to Cross?

WHEN I WAS IN THE FIRST GRADE I DISCOVERED ONE OF LIFE'S TROU-
bling realities. You don't always know to whom you should listen.

Dad drove me to school one morning. In itself that was not
unusual. On this particular day, however, he drove me to the
Acme grocery store across the street from Maple Valley Elementary School. Dad had to pick up some groceries. He parked the
car in the store lot and sent me over to the traffic light at the corner of Copley Road and Hawkins Avenue.

The school crossing guard was on the other side of Hawkins
Avenue, escorting children from the north side of Copley Road
to the school property. Back on my side of the street I nervously
glanced from the crossing guard to Dad to the crossing guard to
Dad again. The light changed. Dad, watching from near the
grocery store door, said, "Go ahead. Cross." Ever desirous of
being obedient, I started to cross. At the same time, ever
desirous of being obedient, I glanced over at the crossing guard.
He was still herding the other children. If I continued to cross I
was afraid he would turn around and see me crossing without
his help. He had come into our classroom often to tell us never

to cross on our own, no matter what color the light. Only cross when he told us to cross.

The crossing guard was a short, jolly man I assumed was nearing retirement age. But his shiny silver badge, yellow belt, and large hand-held stop sign gave him a certain kind of stature that raised in my heart a certain kind of fear. At home I used to make big, red stop signs from oaktag and stand in my driveway pretending to stop cars, so I could feel a bit of the power a crossing guard might possess. I would say to the make-believe children on the other side of the driveway, "Only cross when I tell you to cross!"

But here was Dad. God. Telling me to cross the street when the crossing guard was thirty feet of asphalt away. So I crossed. Dad went into the store, and the guard turned to see me tentatively crossing without his assistance. Rather sternly the usually warm-hearted guard said, "Son, you're not supposed to cross unless I tell you to do so." "But my daddy told me to," I pleaded. As if I hadn't spoken he scolded me again, "Don't ever cross until I tell you to cross." In tears I took my conflicted six-year-old being into Maple Valley Elementary School.

Later that morning the crossing guard stuck his head through our classroom door. He asked the teacher if he could address the class. He reminded the class yet again that we should never cross the street unless he told us to do so. From my seat in the back row I interrupted, "But my daddy told me to." The crossing guard said, "Yes, you should always listen to your father. You have a good daddy. I've talked with him often. But you should listen to me too."

And on that confusing morning I discovered the way is not always easy to know. You should cross when your father tells you to cross. But you shouldn't cross unless the crossing guard says it's okay to cross. And if the two of them don't happen to be working together on your particular crossing dilemma, then what will you do?

The Bard understood the problem. He also had a solution: "To thine own self be true." But youngsters don't yet have much of a self to whom they can be true. They are torn this way and that. Ultimately it's Mom and Dad whose sense of crossing usually wins. That's a terrifying thing to come to know as a father. It's up to me to help my children find their own selves, to identify that to which they can be true. It's up to me to help them discover the touchstone from which they can begin their journeys. And a little more is on the line than a safe crossing to Maple Valley Elementary School. God help me.

You created us in your image, almighty God. You could have scripted every line of our lives if you so chose, but instead of hoarding the power for yourself, you entrusted it to us. You allow us the freedom to make our own decisions, to create our own paths. Grant us the wisdom to know when to cross and when not to cross. And help us to understand when and when not to encourage others to do the same. AMEN.

4

"Carmen" and Other Surprises of Wonder

MY GRADE SCHOOL YEARS SEEM ALL GATHERED TOGETHER IN A single memory. It smells of oiled wood floors and heavily perfumed teachers in their early sixties. Only a couple of specific events stand out. One is from kindergarten. Alaska had just become a state. I stood outside with my classmates while the sixth graders ceremoniously lowered the forty-eight-star flag and put up the new forty-nine-star flag that had been given to our elementary school by the father of a classmate. It's a pleasant enough memory but nowhere near as distinctive as my favorite memory from those grade school years, the fourth-grade field trip to hear the Cleveland Symphony Orchestra under the direction of Mr. Robert Shaw.

All the fourth-grade classes piled into cars driven by classroom mothers and traveled in a convoy to the largest auditorium in town—the sanctuary of the Cathedral of Tomorrow Church. There we joined more than a thousand other fourth graders for a concert by the renowned Cleveland Symphony Orchestra. Our teacher told us we were fortunate to be able to see the famous conductor, Robert Shaw.

The controls on our old stove at home had "Robert Shaw" engraved on their ceramic faces. I wondered if Mr. Shaw made stoves when he wasn't directing the orchestra. I also made the assumption he was the same Robert Shaw who had his own chorale. I used to love their recording of "Sometimes I Feel Like a Motherless Child." But here he was in the flesh. The music wasn't coming through the speakers of the hi-fi. The music was live, and Mr. Shaw was conducting.

The music was Bizet's *Carmen,* and I was filled with wonder and joy. I went home and listened to the music over and over on a long-playing album we had in the back corner of the hi-fi cabinet. I hadn't listened to the album before, but now that I'd heard the same music live, I wouldn't turn it off. I closed my eyes and imagined I was back in the auditorium as I played the album day after day. I would pretend to be Mr. Robert Shaw, bowing before the audience, then turning to the orchestra, raising his hands, and creating wonder.

Early one morning I was in my office reading the *New York Times.* When I turned to the obituary page there was his name and picture—Robert Shaw. The article told of his long and illustrious career and quoted many people who spoke of his brilliance. As I read the obituary my eyes moistened a bit. Surprised at my reaction, I allowed my mind to wander back to the fourth grade, when I was surprised by wonder as I discovered a kind of beauty I had never imagined existed in this world.

Over the years many people have come into my life with their batons, bringing wonder. The Sunday school teacher who taught me to pray. The radio station owner who took a chance and gave a sixteen-year-old a job as an announcer. The engineer who recorded the first album of our fledgling singing group. The philosophy professor who took the time to teach me to think. And yes, the orchestra conductor who brought wonder to at least one fourth-grade boy.

We should celebrate more those who bring wonder into our lives. We should write them notes, leave messages on their answering machines, and tell others of their good deeds. And we should gladly welcome a tear when they are no longer walking among us with their special brand of inspiration.

Lord God, what a wonder you are. Knowing your love, it is little wonder you share so freely of yourself and in so doing allow others to reflect your light into our eyes. Give us courage and open hearts to become reflectors of wonder for the sake of you. AMEN.

5

A Third of a Century, and Then ...

I THOUGHT I MADE MY GRANDFATHER DIE.

I had a pet rabbit. His name was Lightning, and he was one of a succession of pet rabbits. One was run over by a car. Dad didn't tell me until I was twenty-three years old. He always said, "I dunno, Paul, he just got out of the cage and ran away." Yeah, right, Dad.

We donated another rabbit, Cotton, to the Akron Zoo after it scratched my arm and left a scar I can see to this day. The zoo had a rabbit village. Cotton went with the other rabbits into the little rabbit church where they put the feed. I liked the idea of being fed in church.

Lightning didn't get a chance to chow down on feed at the little rabbit church. One Saturday morning I came downstairs, and Dad called me from the basement. "Paul, I have some bad news. Lightning died." There was no apparent cause of death. He just died. But as I walked away from the house toward Pritchard's Drug Store that morning, prepared to drown my grief in a nickel's worth of candy, I worked a ten-year-old's sad magic.

I knew Papa, my dad's father, was sick. Dad had told me about the cancer around Christmas time. I vaguely understood the illness was terminal. But I didn't have a very good handle on exactly what that meant. I only knew at some point in the not too distant future I would have to experience the same emptiness in the pit of my stomach I had felt five months earlier when Mom's father had died. The same feeling I was having now, at the corner of Roslyn and Maple, as I walked to the drug store. Moving across the concrete squares, taking care not to step on a single crack, I thought the thought out loud. "If Lightning has to die, then Papa might as well die." There. I said it. I prayed it. Then I stepped on a crack. And a few days later Papa died. Just as I had prayed.

I dared not talk to a soul about it. And through all the activity of the funeral I didn't give it much conscious thought. But then we were back in Akron. No Papa. No Lightning. Just the fears of a ten-year-old boy that maybe he had prayed a terrible prayer that an awful God had answered.

I never did talk with anyone about it. I grieved, trudging unknowingly through the cycles of denial, anger, bargaining, depression, and acceptance. Every now and then I remembered what happened at the corner of Roslyn and Maple, but I pushed it aside. I grew up, and the faded and torn memory was relegated to some cobwebbed corner of my heart.

Then came the day my graduate professor read aloud how the Holy Spirit prays for us when we cannot pray for ourselves. And I was taken back to the corner of Roslyn and Maple, and my eyes welled with tears. There had been someone translating for me on that cold April morning. The words from my mouth had reached the ears of God wet with the tears of the Spirit. "Protect this little one, who knows only of dying and does not yet understand the other side."

A couple of years ago we were driving through Ohio. After getting gas at a station just off the interstate, I looked across the highway to a large cemetery on a hill. Even though I didn't know the location of the cemetery in which my grandfather was buried, I had a sense this serene spot in the gently rolling hills of

eastern Ohio was his final resting place. I had been there only
once, on an April day in 1961. Yet here it was, the summer of
1994, and I was confident an unhealed memory was nearby.

Over the mild protestations of my family I headed into the
cemetery and drove around until I found a place that felt right. I
stopped the car, got out, and started walking past the grave-
stones. There were no standing marble and granite headstones.
All the markers were flat against the ground. I walked about
thirty feet, looked at about ten or fifteen markers, and then my
heart caught in my throat. There were my grandparents' graves. I
fell to my knees and sobbed. My children retreated to the car.
My wife came and touched my shoulders. I pulled weeds away
from the marker with my hands. I touched the stone and traced
the letters. I had not been to that spot in a third of a century. I
had never asked where the grave was. I hadn't wanted to know.

Now, the stone wet with tears, I finally forgave myself for that
child's prayer. And I thanked God that the Spirit speaks for us
the words we do not know to speak and that death is not the
final word.

*Heavenly Father, thank you for sending your Spirit to be present with
us, healing our wounds, cleansing our memories, and accompanying us
on the hills and valleys of this ever so twisting journey. AMEN.*

6

Just Okay Chicken

I'VE ALWAYS HEARD THAT HE WAS NOT A PARTICULARLY GRACEFUL man. I've seen videotapes of interviews done with him in his later years. I would call the language colorful. And his spirit—a bit on the aggressive side. Which seemed odd to me, because his public image was one of Southern gentility.

You have to understand, my mother was from Kentucky. Bluegrass country to be exact. She was the third child of a humble and good tenant farmer. Most of the folks I knew from Kentucky were good and gentle. I was surprised, therefore, when I discovered this particular Southern gentleman was not such a gentle man.

I loved fried chicken. It was food for the soul. No doubt my love for chicken was in the Kentucky part of my genes. Grandma's fried chicken was the best, and after that Mom's, and way, way after that, the fried chicken of everyone else. But still I was open to trying new versions of my favorite food. And we were all intrigued with the new sit-down restaurant that had come to our neck of the woods. "Kentucky Fried Chicken," said the big bold red sign in front of the shopping center restaurant. It was the grand opening, and we went after church on Sunday. The chicken was okay. Just okay.

About halfway through the meal a Cadillac pulled up to the shopping center curb, and a white-haired man dressed in a white suit emerged. The staff inside said it was Colonel Sanders. Since he looked a lot like the man on the big bold red sign, I assumed he was the owner. And yes, it was the Colonel Sanders. In the flesh. Goatee, cane, and all. He came to our table, and Mom told him she was from Bourbon County, Kentucky. We didn't realize it at the time, but the Colonel wasn't from Kentucky. He was from Indiana. But "Indiana Fried Chicken" would never do. He smiled, and acted like he knew where Bourbon County was, and asked how we liked the chicken. We kind of lied and said it was great, because we had learned to be polite, no matter what the circumstances. And then Colonel Sanders was gone.

It's now forty years later. Colonel Sanders has been dead for quite some time, although the advertising folks seem to have resurrected him of late. And me? I've been a Kentucky colonel for the past ten years. That's right. I have a friend who was the assistant secretary of state of Kentucky, and he made me a Kentucky colonel. I have the declaration somewhere in my house. I haven't started any restaurants though.

Grandma's been gone for almost twenty years, and Mom doesn't fry chicken much any more. I count fat grams now and haven't been to a Kentucky Fried Chicken restaurant in about ten years. I have lived in New York for twenty-five years. For most of that time I've tried to be a gentle man, much like those many Kentucky gentlemen I remember from my youth. On most days I can still remember the taste of Grandma's and Mom's fried chicken, seasoned with plenty of gentleness and goodness and chock full of enough love to keep a Kentucky boy well nourished in the northland.

God who is in the small things, help us remember that stories told at bedtime, tears dried by a loving hand, games of catch in the backyard, and meals of fried chicken are more lasting than the most successful of business ventures. AMEN.

7

A Christmas Remembered

IT WAS THE CHRISTMAS SEASON, AND I WAS IN GRADE SCHOOL. After I'D had two years of learning basic German taught in a northern Ohio accent over a school loudspeaker, Mom considered me ready to sing "Silent Night" in my newfound tongue.

It was a Sunday evening service. With white shirt, clip-on tie, and red sweater, I marched up to the second pew, pushed forward by Mom. We'd never sat there before. We usually sat respectably toward the middle, like all the other church leaders. We seldom sat in the absolute back unless I was sick and Mom thought she might have to take me out in the middle of the service. But there we sat in the second row.

We sang Christmas carols, and Dad asked for favorites. He was the minister, after all. Others could lead singing, but only Dad was authorized to ask for favorites. Then came the communion hymn. About every third week it was "Tis Midight and on Olive's Brow." I wasn't exactly sure what the song meant, but I loved listening to it. Even as a child I was haunted by the last line, "The suffering Savior prays, alone." As the song was being sung, those who had missed the morning communion service would come down and sit in the first pew. After they had received communion we sang again, and they returned to their seats. A lot of them worked the morning shift at the tire factory.

Communion completed, Dad announced the special music. I stood by the piano, and the introduction began. I saw all those people, larger than life, and I saw my mother, sitting there in the wrong place in the second pew. My brother was giggling on the back row with two of his friends, and I whispered the words "Stille Nacht, Hei . . . ," and that's as far as I got. I shot out the side door of the Noble Avenue Church in anything but a spirit of nobility. I stood crying in the hallway wishing I could somehow make the whole season disappear.

Dad preached, and for twenty minutes I stood at the door and watched. Dad secretly gestured from behind the pulpit, trying to coax me from the doorway to a seat in the sanctuary. But the doorway was my sanctuary, and I wouldn't budge.

The service was over, and everybody but a couple of families had gone home. I finally ventured back into the sanctuary. My big brother was still in the back, snickering. Dad was shaking hands with his best preacher smile, and Mom was talking with the wife of one of the elders. They both had an eye on me.

An older woman came up and gave me a hug. Dad walked down the aisle and put his arm on my shoulder, and we walked to the car. Not a word was spoken. We stopped at the corner store, and he bought me a pack of wintergreen Life Savers.

I've spoken and sung many times since, even to crowds of thousands. I still get nervous, but I haven't run out of any doors lately. I've felt like it a few times, but I keep speaking and do the best I can do on that particular occasion, given my humanity. People often say nice things to me after I've finished speaking, and I always appreciate their kind words. But I have to admit all those kind words combined have never meant as much to me as that single pack of wintergreen Life Savers.

The greatest gift of all came on a silent and holy night. Through that gift even the smallest of gifts can have the most profound meaning. Thank you, God of Christmas remembered, for bringing love to earth, to be tasted and felt and known. AMEN.

8

A Hero in Eastern Kentucky

ERNIE'S CLAIM TO FAME WAS THAT HE WAS A COUSIN OF ROY Rogers. You could tell they had a common ancestry. The resemblance was in the eyes. And you never forgot Ernie's eyes.

The last time I saw Ernie he was ravaged by Alzheimer's. Sitting in the same chair he used to sit in when I would watch him fall asleep during Cincinnati Reds games, he had a vacant stare coming from those still graceful eyes. When his wife, Mary Lucy, was in the kitchen getting me some iced tea, I spoke to Ernie from my heart, thanking him for his life and for his grace.

One of the earliest memories I have of Ernie is from my grade school years. We often visited my mother's hometown in eastern Kentucky, and I saw Ernie at the grocery store he operated on the west end of Main Street. I could tell Dad liked him from the lilt in Dad's voice when he called out Ernie's name. I loved to hear Ernie talk. He had a marked Southern accent that seemed to speak of all that is good and gentle in the foothills of eastern Kentucky.

Years later Ernie opened Womack's Five and Ten in the heart of the business district. That's where I found him when we moved to town during my sophomore year of high school. I started spending a lot of time with his son and a lot of time hanging out in the store. For a few weeks during the spring of my tenth-grade year, I started staying in the store all day on Saturdays to help, uninvited. One rainy Saturday Ernie gently told me I wouldn't be needed, and I slinked out of the store, more than a little embarrassed for my pushy ways. When his family later headed on vacation to Myrtle Beach, Ernie asked for my assistance in the store, and I felt forgiven and redeemed.

During the week Ernie was on vacation one of his World War II buddies came by. They had spent a good bit of time together flying over Europe during the war, and he hadn't seen Ernie since. He was disappointed to have missed him. He lingered in the store for a while and talked warmly of Ernie's companionship and encouragement as they struggled through World War II.

When I graduated from college and began working for a youth organization, I had to raise my financial support. Ernie was the first to make a commitment. My first Christmas home after moving away I was reminded of another of his quiet gifts. I watched as Ernie, my father, and others filled the church Christmas bags that year. The church always handed out bags filled with candy at Christmas time. Always white lunch-size bags, heavy with orange slices, chocolate drops, and other assorted goodies. Ernie sold the candy to the church at a suspiciously low price. His good works were done in secret.

An older gentleman lived alone in a trailer on a hillside just north of town. He had a developmental disability, but he was able to care for himself, more or less, with a little help from the kindness of those in town. Everyone knew him, but he had a way of showing up at Ernie's a little more often than most anywhere else. A chicken dinner or a bag of candy was always at the ready as a gift from Ernie's family.

Ernie was an elder at the church. He didn't talk about the gospel so much as he did the gospel. His wife had her own quiet grace. They were both too kind for their earthly good. I still enjoy stopping by to speak with her whenever I visit my hometown.

The conversations are full of goodness and values you can build a culture on. And their children? Those apples didn't fall too far from the tree. Good people, all of them.

I was working in Tennessee and didn't get to attend Ernie's funeral. I'm sorry I couldn't go. Just to have had the chance to honor him one more time would have been good for my heart. He might have been Roy Rogers's cousin, but Roy wasn't the hero of my youth. Ernie was.

In Genesis you tell us not to be afraid, for you are with us. Open our eyes, Lord, to your presence in the lives of those who walk among us. Open our hearts to the people who are filled not with themselves but with your love. And give us the strength to be like them. AMEN.

9

A Father's Mercy

WHEN I WAS IN HIGH SCHOOL I WAS FORTUNATE ENOUGH TO secure a position as an announcer at the one and only local radio station. The station played a variety of music from bluegrass to rock and roll and billed itself as "Your Variety Station." We covered local politics, reported on prices at the fall tobacco warehouse sales, and provided live, play-by-play coverage of county high school basketball games. The play-by-play coverage is where this story begins.

During the Christmas season of my senior year I was assigned to travel to the west end of the county to call the first game of a double-header. Someone else would call the second game since I had to drive home and get to bed and sign the station on the air at six the next morning. I borrowed Dad's green 1966 Chevrolet Bel Air, collected my friend from his front porch down below Main Street, and headed west on U.S. 60.

A few hours later, with the game over and my mind already moving on to the very early morning before me, I walked back to the car. It was blocked on three sides by cars that had arrived for the second game. On the fourth side the car was a few inches from a portable cement mixer attached to a trailer hitch. I could either wait until the second game was over at about eleven, or I could try to maneuver my way out. With my friend guiding me and sweat pouring off my brow because the car had no power steering, I carefully moved the Chevy back and forth until I maneuvered away from the three cars. Assuming I was home free, I put my foot on the gas and heard an ominous thud. I had caught the front left fender of Dad's car on the trailer hitch of that portable cement mixer. My friend went around to the front of the car and assessed the damage. I rolled down the window.

"Do you think Dad will notice?" I asked. My friend answered, "Unless your father has lost his sight in the last three hours, he's gonna notice." I got out of the car and stared at the softball-sized dent in the front left fender.

The next day I drove to the radio station very early in the morning and then drove home at noon. I parked the car way, way back behind the garage, distancing myself from my offense. I offered no explanations and waited for Dad's inquisition to begin. All afternoon Dad asked no questions. That evening he took Mom to dinner at one of their favorite restaurants about twenty miles away. When he got home, still no queries. I figured he was waiting until after church on Sunday morning, giving guilt its best effect. But after church services on Sunday there were no questions from Dad, and, of course, no explanations offered by me. A week later, still not a word. A month later the softball-sized dent in the front left fender was fixed.

It is thirty-one years later, and though it took me a while to understand, I think I'm finally coming to the conclusion my father has chosen to be merciful toward the younger of his two sons. It wouldn't be the first time a father has responded with such marvelous mercy.

Lord God of all mercy, thank you for forgiving the dents we put in your creation now and again. May we live ever grateful for your marvelous grace. And may we reflect that grace to the lives of others. AMEN.

10

Knowing One Place

THERE IS A VERY LEAN HIKER WHO HAS CLIMBED MT. MONADNOCK in southern New Hampshire every day for more than seven years. I was at the top of Monadnock last June. It was probably my seventh or eighth time up the mountain. After an hour and a half of tripping over roots and scrambling up granite slabs we arrived at the summit. Lots of other people were there too. Monadnock is the second most climbed mountain in the world. Mt. Fuji is first. Because of the large numbers of hikers, we take a circuitous, seldom-used route. It takes longer, but the solitude on the journey is blessed.

When we arrived at the round metal disk some government employee had hammered into the granite signifying the top of the mountain (it's not always as easy as you might think to identify the exact top), there he was. Mr. Every Day Climber. He was carrying a walkie-talkie to speak with the rangers at the trailhead, so they could be informed of the day's summit conditions. New England was green as far as the eye could behold. I have to admit I'm partial to hiking in the Rockies. There are fewer bugs, and nothing is more beautiful than an alpine meadow. But as beautiful as the Rockies are, you can't beat the summertime views from a New England peak. Those same trees that produced a root-tripping journey on the way up stretch out like velvet from the Berkshires of Massachusetts to the Green Mountains of Vermont to the legendary Whites of northern New Hampshire.

I didn't talk with Mr. Every Day Climber, but my hiking partner did. Mr. Every Day said sure enough, he was the guy, and he had to get down pretty soon to go to work. Not exactly an inspiring conversation.

There is a wisdom that comes from knowing one place. I imagine Mr. Every Day knows every inch of the trip up Monadnock, regardless of the trail he chooses on any particular day. He knows the subtle changes in the colors below, the exact spot where the skyscrapers of Boston can be seen on a clear morning, the names of the peaks in southern Vermont. There are probably specific maple roots on the route that have become respected obstacles on his journey. Particularly slippery slabs of granite that hold warmth on a clear fall day and misery in a January nor'easter. Mr. Every Day knows that mountain.

My paternal grandfather lived on the left or right banks of the Ohio River all of his working days. A similar life was lived by my maternal grandfather in eastern Kentucky. While he spent his "retirement years" working in Carter County, a whopping eighty miles from his birthplace, most of his life was spent in Bourbon County. Both were men who knew the wisdom of living in one place. In the guest beds in their homes I would lie awake at night, listening to each tell stories of his neck of the woods. They climbed the same mountain, so to speak, for decades upon decades. One a farmer. The other a railroad worker.

And me? I just sat in a MD-80 for an hour while they replaced the starter in the starboard engine. It was eighty-something outside and felt like a hundred-something inside. I fly enough to know MD-80s can't produce adequate air conditioning on the ground. 737s—a different story. A-319s—perfect, thank you. And F-100s have a peculiar air conditioning system. Take off on a hot day and it sounds like someone opened a bag of rice in the overhead compartments. It's ice flowing through the air conditioning ducts, they say. I think someone lets open a bag of rice in the overhead compartments.

And why do I take this short detour to airplane cooling technologies? Because it's what I know. I fly over the Ohio River. I don't live on the banks of it like Papa Williams did. I cover the eighty miles between Bourbon County and Carter County in about twelve minutes. It took Pa Stone two hours to drive it over one-lane roads.

I fly into Manchester, New Hampshire, for a meeting in the morning, a hike in the afternoon, and a short night's rest. The next morning it's off to the next day's time zone. I fly more than a hundred thousand miles a year. I don't have the wisdom that comes from knowing one place. I have the wisdom that comes from knowing one airline. Somehow it doesn't compare.

I'm not optimistic about a nation that teaches its men and women to have no roots. In my grandfather's generation fathers passed their work to their sons. On average, my father's generation had one career and two jobs. My generation has two careers and six jobs. Pundits tell me my children's generation will have up to six careers and twenty jobs. Not exactly putting down roots, and not particularly conducive to serving a community or nurturing our spouses and children.

Both grandfathers led difficult lives. Nothing came easy. No free first-class upgrades. No February trips to Disney World. But they did have the wisdom that comes from knowing one place. And as I gaze out the window of 1A to the bluegrass of central Kentucky below, it gets me thinking. This morning I was in West Palm Beach. Tonight I'll be in Indianapolis, and tomorrow Louisville, and Tuesday New York. And you know what? I'm envious of my grandfathers.

For forty years your people wandered the wilderness, Lord, never quite knowing that wherever you are is home. In the busyness of these times, may we ever be aware our true home is with the God who packs his bags and journeys with us. AMEN.

11

My Network Debut

I CALLED MY ADMINISTRATIVE ASSISTANT FROM MY CELLULAR PHONE on a Tuesday afternoon. "I saw you on television last night," she said. A new national television network had kicked off at two that afternoon, and a Christian network with which I'm affiliated was running its programming during the overnight hours, between 1 and 6 a.m. As one of the devotional hosts for that network, my videotaped debut aired at 1:30 a.m. I wasn't up.

I was going to watch the next night from my hotel room in Denver, but my programming wasn't on until 3:30 that morning, and insomnia has never been a problem of mine. The rest of the week I was busy hiking with friends, reading, writing. It was about two months before I finally saw a segment. It was okay, I guess, but it didn't seem like something worth staying up for.

I've been on the air for a couple years now. I get a lot of help. For the last several months we've had a new director who has worked on a number of films, and the network's programming vice-president has been a wellspring of ideas and a kind and gentle coach. Both have helped me understand my gestures need to be "smaller" on camera than they are before a live audience. They also tell me my facial expressions ought to be a little less exaggerated. Evidently the more "takes" I attempt, the stiffer I get. They try to be happy with the second or third "take."

The Board of Stewards of the network didn't want "seasoned" television hosts. They wanted "real" people who live and work in a "real" world. With that explanation I accepted their offer to host as a compliment. I like being thought of as "real."

I'm still a novice, but those in charge tell me I'm getting a little better. The director and programming vice-president are both great storytellers themselves, and they are partial to the stories I tell. I must admit I'm partial to them myself. Every now and then someone will come up to me on a street or at the airport and thank me for encouraging them in the middle of the night. I'm pleased by that. I wouldn't mind being remembered for having provided a little encouragement in the middle of the night.

On our better days we might be able to do something to bring a little reconciliation and encouragement to the world. On our better days.

God of co-mission, I understand you could get along fine without my help. But I need to be reminded that I need the work. I need the joy of purpose. Thank you for gifting me with this awesome co-ministry with you, reconciling the creation to the Creator. AMEN.

12

A Glad-Hearted Day

IT WAS A TIME RESERVED FOR GRIEF AND MOURNING, BUT IT FELT
more like a glad-hearted day.

My uncle died last week. He lived to see the first couple weeks
of the new millennium, finished dinner one evening, then went
off to see his Maker.

After the visitation the night before the funeral, my cousin
told me a couple of days before my uncle died he couldn't get to
sleep. He asked the nursing home attendant to give him the
remote control so he could watch television. He turned to the
channel where I serve as a program host and watched me on television. She said he watched all night long. It's not that he
wanted to watch all night, mind you. He couldn't find the
remote control to turn off the television.

It was late at night after the visitation when my oldest cousin
told that story. We were in another cousin's kitchen sitting around
the table with my uncle's three daughters. We laughed heartily as
we had all evening long. You see, my uncle was a good and decent
man. And when a good and decent man dies just shy of his
eighty-fifth birthday, it is a time for a glad-hearted day.

My uncle was the president of a college in eastern Kentucky. He
took the helm at twenty-two, when his father the founder died,
and he served faithfully for the next four decades. The school is
my alma mater. I studied the history of Western civilization with
my uncle when I was a freshman. I was often confident I had

answers, but he was gracious enough to spare me the news that I didn't even know the questions. He often admitted that he didn't either, and somehow that made him a teacher to be trusted.

My uncle was a man of few words, with a dry humor and a wry smile. Like many native eastern Kentuckians he wasn't given to the use of unnecessary adjectives. Nouns and verbs, thank you. When asked to give a reference for someone, he was often inclined to answer, "When you know him like I know him you'll appreciate him like I appreciate him." You never much knew what he was thinking. His humility and faithfulness were much appreciated. He worked tirelessly and selflessly day after day, year after year.

I remember when we needed to print tickets for my senior play in high school. My uncle accompanied us to the college administration building, created the stencil, and printed the tickets, one at a time. I tried to make conversation, but it was pretty one-sided. He listened a lot and smiled a little, and I wondered what he was thinking turning that crank printing those tickets.

The visitation and funeral were, as you might expect, heartwarming affairs. Throughout the college chapel groups of nephews and nieces huddled together discussing the state of the church, magazine articles, promising young ministers, the NFL playoffs, and life in eastern Kentucky. Professors and students from the college came and went, as well as leaders from town. The quietly satisfying occasion was proof positive that a life lived for others has great rewards.

At his funeral the concert choir sang "Great Is Thy Faithfulness." At my aunt's funeral years earlier they had sung "It Is Well with My Soul." Two grand hymns for two grand saints.

Faithfulness and well souls. Lives lived steadfastly toward the right. Daughters with fine memories of a father who loved and a Father who loves. Now there's a reason for a glad-hearted day.

Lord of the resurrection, we praise you that death is not the final word and that at the end of the day you are the one left standing. And you stand, and stand there, and stand. AMEN.

At Home

1

On Seeing Eyes

I HAD BEEN AWAKE SINCE ABOUT 6 A.M., AND I HAD NOT EATEN since breakfast. It was very late, and I was hungry.

There were several twenty-two-hour McDonald's restaurants around Buffalo. The stores closed from 3 to 5 a.m. They were open the other twenty-two hours of the day. It was about 2:45 a.m. when I floated into the store on Transit Road.

I remember it vividly because an hour and a half earlier a door had opened, and I had first looked into the eyes of my firstborn son, Jonathan. As I stood in line to order my Quarter Pounder I was sure the surprisingly large number of customers, considering the hour, could all tell this tall, lean, polyester-shirted twenty-five-year-old was a new father.

As I took the sandwich into my hands and thought of the life-changing events of the day, I choked up before I could take my first bite. All I could see were those newborn eyes trying too hard to focus. Only a few minutes earlier at Millard Fillmore Suburban Hospital I had been mesmerized by those eyes. I wanted to help them focus, point them in the right direction, encourage their gaze. I wanted them to look like they had been expecting me. But as I focused my eyes on the most beautiful sight they had ever beheld, Jonathan's eyes crossed and wandered around the room, focusing on nothing in particular.

Those first hundred hours or so brought unspeakable joy side by side with genuine fear. How could I encourage this child of God to love his Creator? How could I help those bright blue eyes find their focus? What did I know about fatherhood?

Those same feelings came to me on two more occasions. As I stood in the outdoor observation area at New York's John F. Kennedy Airport, I watched the Air India 747 that was bringing our infant daughter, Jael, execute a missed approach. What if my fathering turned out to include too many missed approaches? My stomach ached again as I sat in the wrong lobby waiting at the wrong telephone for the obstetrician's call that my wife's Cesarian section was over and that our second daughter, Jana, had been born. They finally found me and gave me the good news, but I wondered how many more times in Jana's life I would be at the wrong place at the wrong time.

Jana is graduating from high school next Saturday. Then she will go off to college in Philadelphia. Jael, my daughter from India, is going back upstate to begin her sophomore year of college. Jonathan is working hard at his summer job, saving money for his senior year of college in Colorado.

I gave up Quarter Pounders about eight years ago. There are no more twenty-two-hour McDonald's. But I still get choked up taking bites of life. And I still struggle with how best to encourage my children to love their Creator and to find their focus. I pray I'll be looking into the eyes of my children until these eyes see no more. And I pray they can take from this father's eyes enough love to move forward on the journey as they learn to focus more and more clearly on the Father who misses no approaches.

Heavenly Father, we love so much these tender hearts you have entrusted to our care. Give us gentle hands, warm love, and eyes turned steadfastly toward the right as we give them wings to fly. AMEN.

2

In the Loving Arms of Her Father

WE HAD ADOPTED OUR DAUGHTER JAEL FROM CALCUTTA, INDIA, three years earlier. With hollow eyes and frighteningly skinny arms and legs she arrived on an Air India flight on a chilly November evening. The early days were difficult. Jael was on a special formula that cost nine dollars a can, and a can lasted less than two days. A few minutes of sleep here and there were all she managed as she struggled to survive. There were frequent trips to two young doctors who provided superb care and later became good friends.

Three years later Jael was healthy and chock full of life as we drove to the CNN studios in Manhattan. Just a few days earlier the Mission in Calcutta that had nurtured our daughter's life and delivered her safely to us was told to cease operations until authorities could get to the bottom of a British newspaper story accusing the organization of selling sick babies for profit.

The story was most offensive, twisting the facts about an infant who had died from Sudden Infant Death Syndrome after adoptive placement. The adoptive parents were angry with the reporter, and with just cause. The story got CNN's attention, and they interviewed the author of the spurious article in a talk show. They also interviewed me. Hence the trip to Manhattan. My daughter was accompanying me because the producers wanted their viewers to see a different side of the story.

Faced with a happy child brimming with life because of the sacrifices of the Mission in India, the author of the article broke into a profuse sweat. The interviewer relentlessly tore at his motives, and there was some delight watching him squirm. Time and again the camera would focus on my grinning daughter, playing comfortably in her father's lap, while the interviewer grilled the reporter about endangering the lives of children like these by writing such a wrong-headed article.

The interview worked its magic. Within a couple of days the Mission was cleared and adoptions were again joyfully completed. I never read another article by the reporter, although I wouldn't be surprised if he is writing for a supermarket tabloid somewhere. But I remember what the CNN reporter told me that night when the show was over. With a wink and a grin she said, "The smile of your child in the loving arms of her father was what unnerved that reporter the most and what gave this show its real power."

I suppose that's always where the real power lies. In the smile of a child resting in the loving arms of his or her father. Spurious articles don't stand too tall in the face of embodied truth. Love in a lap, for all to see and know.

Snatching us up from malnourishment, you nurture us with your love, God, inviting us to rest, play, and enjoy life wrapped in your loving arms. AMEN.

3

Christmas Gifts and Hard Lessons

MOST FAMILIES ENJOY MARVELOUSLY UNIQUE CHRISTMAS TRADITIONS. When I was a young child our family was no exception. One of the traditions in the Williams household included wrapping all Christmas presents except for the "big" gift. That was unopened, unwrapped, and proudly displayed beneath the Christmas tree on Christmas morning.

One Christmas in the early 1960s Mom and Dad left my gift opened, as usual, next to the Christmas tree. It was a bright red twenty-six-inch bicycle, with headlight, saddlebags, and white sidewall tires. When I ran down the steps and saw it taking up all that space in front of the Christmas tree, I was elated.

My older brother had a fairly inexpensive tennis racket lying under the tree. He didn't realize his major gift, a ping-pong table, was in the dining room. He tried to be excited for me and for his inexpensive tennis racket, but you could tell he was working hard. As soon as Mom and Dad realized he hadn't seen the ping-pong table in the other room, they hurried him in, and with great relief he realized Christmas had arrived. I could tell Mom and Dad felt badly they hadn't seen his disappointment sooner and more quickly pointed him in the direction of the dining room. But they recovered nicely, and the excitement of Christmas was saved.

When my son was in the first grade, his elementary school had a special Christmas gift program for the children. Volunteers, mostly grandparents, helped the children with a special in-school store, where the students could buy modest gifts for Mom and Dad without Mom and Dad knowing the gift that had been chosen. Jonathan proudly picked out his gift for Mom, had it wrapped by one of the grandparent volunteers at the holiday sale, and brought it home.

Fourteen days later it was Christmas morning, and Jonathan watched with eager anticipation as his mother opened her gift. As she tore off the paper his eyes widened in horror as his mom pulled out a Christmas plant, brown as brown could be, and quite dead. It seemed the grandparent volunteer had failed to inform Jonathan the gift needed to be watered and therefore given and unwrapped immediately. Jonathan burst into tears and ran into his room. He seemed to get over it within a few minutes, but Mom and Dad were not so fortunate. We both still get tears in our eyes when we think back to that Christmas. To tell the truth, it's the only thing we remember about that particular year's celebration. For it was one of the first times one of our children had to discover no matter how hard you try, sometimes life doesn't work out the way you want.

It was also one of the first times we realized how difficult it is to watch your own child encounter one of life's hard lessons. And the older they grew, the tougher the lessons, and the harder it became to stand by and suffer with them. We came to know there is a price you pay when you love someone dearly and suffering pays its inevitable call, even when its arrival is ushered in by something as small as a dead Christmas plant.

I can only imagine how God feels when I suffer. And when he watched his suffering Son?

How many tears you must have shed, dear Lord? You know the hurts I have known. You know the heartaches I have felt. And you walk through the dark nights with me, and with my son, and with my daughter, and with my other daughter, and with my wife, and with my next-door neighbor, and with the grandparent volunteer at the elementary school. How can you bear the pain, dear Lord, except that you know what lies on the other side of the darkness? Give me the hope, Lord, of the other side. AMEN.

4

Pathmark Neapolitan Ice Cream

MY DAUGHTERS, JAEL AND JANA, WERE ABOUT FOUR AND THREE years of age the day they approached my study. With two very different personalities the girls were not exactly inseparable. In fact, until they reached their high school years and became good friends they seldom agreed on much of anything. On this particular occasion, however, they were of one accord.

Jael came hopefully into the room. "Daddy, could we have some ice cream?" Jana stood at the top of the steps, with only her blonde hair and one bright eye showing from behind the doorjamb. "Girls," I replied, "it's much too close to dinnertime for ice cream. Mom will be home soon, and we'll have dinner. Then we'll talk about dessert." Quickly and obediently they departed. That was my clue something was amiss. Usually they would have passionately pleaded their case, always cognizant of the reality that Dad was more likely to give in than Mom. But not this time. They left. I cocked an ear.

"Hurry!" Jael whispered. "Don't let Dad hear." I waited until I figured they were about half finished with the forbidden ice cream, then in a stage voice I called, "Well, I'm done studying. I think I'll go upstairs now." They scrambled. "Hide it," I heard Jana cry, as I walked up the steps.

When I entered the room both girls were seated at the kitchen table coloring the same picture. It was the first and last time I ever saw them share a coloring page. In the sink were two half-finished bowls of Pathmark brand Neapolitan ice cream. I thought, "Wow, one would figure they would have hidden the ice cream more imaginatively than that. Those bowls of ice cream are in plain sight." But then I realized their perspective. To a three-year-old and a four-year-old, the big high sink is a place that leaves its contents quite out of their line of sight.

I walked over to both girls and sternly asked, "You didn't have any ice cream, did you?" Jael has beautiful brown skin and big brown eyes. She looked up at me with those brown eyes, with vanilla and strawberry ice cream all over her beautiful brown face, and confidently replied, "No, Daddy, I didn't have any ice cream." To fair-skinned Jana I asked, "Are you sure you didn't have any ice cream?" She kept her head low, coloring her picture. Finally she looked up, mouth covered in chocolate ice cream, and answered with some conviction, "Nope."

Needless to say, both girls didn't get ice cream after dinner that evening. In our house they often heard us say, "Honesty is not the best policy. Honesty is the only policy." The price to pay for their lack of honesty was an evening without ice cream. Big brother got dessert. They watched.

The girls have been less than truthful many times hence. So has their brother. And so has their father. And if you think you are always truthful, look out. You might be in more trouble than you think. The fact is all of us avoid the truth, at least on occasion. Much as we want to be honest we seem to lack the confidence the truth will suffice. Jesus once said it was truth that would set us free. But from our response, you'd think freedom isn't the first item on our wish list.

To the God who wants so deeply to set us free in truth, may we have the courage to follow your way, and to find your life, and to remain steadfastly and always focused on the truth that is you. AMEN.

5

A Game of Redeeming Features

THE METS HAD WON THE 1986 WORLD SERIES, AND EVERYONE wanted season tickets for 1987. When I went to the stadium to choose seats the Mets staff took me to the visitors' locker room, where only recently Bill Buckner had contemplated Mookie Wilson's ball that scooted between his legs. Yeah, Mookie was fast, and he had to hurry, and with those hobbled knees it would be close. But if he had only straightened up after picking up the ball and made a fast toss to the covering pitcher . . .

But it didn't work that way, much to the chagrin of all of New England. After winning that sixth game and coming from behind in the seventh, the Mets won the World Series. Ray Knight, after a key hit in the seventh, deciding game, was speaking about earlier missed opportunities in that final game. He said he was thankful baseball is a game of redeeming features. As I sat in the visitors' locker room that day, studying stadium diagrams and choosing seats for the next season, I knew we Mets fans were grateful baseball is a game of redeeming features.

Just five months later we were in our regular seats in the fourth row, behind the box seats, in the loge section of Shea Stadium. When Howard Johnson was batting left-handed and connected too early there were lots of fly balls right into our section. My son, Jonathan, was ten years old, and on many a night we discussed our plan. We'd given up bringing our gloves to the games, but if a ball did come our way we would take off our baseball caps, catch the ball in the cap, and hold tightly onto the brim and the back of the cap. We hoped that would be enough to keep the ball securely in our grasp. We even tried it at home a time or two. But no balls headed to loge section 23, row D, seats 1 to 4.

And then it came. I don't remember who was pitching, but it was a right-handed pitcher, because Howard Johnson was batting left-handed. With that early swing he sent a rocket our way. People, popcorn, and beer went flying everywhere. Jonathan struggled mightily to get to the ball first, but this loud guy with a Brooklyn accent beat him to it. He thrust the ball into the air for the better part of a week and a half, proudly showing his prize. Later in the game Jonathan fearfully approached to ask if he could see the ball. With a gruff response the Brooklyn-accented fan said, "I'll let you hold it, kid, but you're not going to try to run with it, are you?" Jonathan held the ball in awe, and after about 2.3 nanoseconds Mr. Brooklyn took it back. We got close to other baseballs during the ten years we had the tickets, but never that close.

Jonathan is twenty-two now and a senior in college. He attends a school in Denver, and the Mets were in town to play the Rockies. The Mets were in the middle of a pennant race, and Jonathan was fortunate enough to get two tickets. He invited a friend to attend the game with him. When they were ushered to their seats, Jonathan noted they were in a good location for a foul ball and reminisced about the man from Brooklyn. And then it came. It bounced once and landed at his feet. Jonathan reached down and snatched it up.

Then he turned around and handed it to the little kid behind him, who was sitting there with his baseball glove and his dreams of a foul ball securely nestled in it. Jonathan told

him the baseball belonged to him. No questions asked. No
explanations given.

Jonathan drove home and went to bed. He got up the next
morning and headed off to class, and then he called to tell me
he'd gotten a foul ball. And that he had given it away to the kid
in the seat behind him. Together we redeemed the memory of a
guy from Brooklyn who did not understand half of what
Jonathan understands about baseball being a game of redeeming features.

*To the God of redeeming features, heal our lives of hurtful memories,
and in the healing may a blessing be poured into the life of another.
AMEN.*

6

Three Empty Rooms

WE TOOK OUR YOUNGEST CHILD, JANA, TO COLLEGE ON SUNDAY. She slept in her Saturn while her mother drove. I drove the Honda and led the way. The trip was relatively quick, about two hours and forty-five minutes. I live near New York City, and you never gauge a trip by miles. You always talk hours and minutes. That two-hour-and-forty-five-minute drive stretched into a four-hour drive on the way home.

When we got to the college we immediately started moving Jana's belongings into the dorm room. We followed the routine we'd learned twice before. I thought it might be easier this time, but it was harder than ever. Jana, always ready to take on the world, was uncharacteristically tentative. She didn't talk much and stood around while we put things in place. Then it was on to the orientation session.

The gymnasium was filled to capacity with students and family members. Administrators gave their speeches. The president, with wit and intelligence, offered timely remarks, and it was time to go. We hurriedly helped our daughter buy some books, and then we were standing in the stairwell hugging her good-bye. She was crying and whispered to me, "I can't stay in this place." I hugged her tight and assured her she was going to be all right. Then I walked to the car and stared straight ahead for a few long seconds.

Tears usually come fairly easily to my eyes. I don't think much
about it; they just arrive, most often appropriately. But this time,
no tears. Just emptiness. I hardly talked to my wife on the very
long trip home. I just yelled, sometimes under my breath and
sometimes not, at all the stupid drivers, the stupid highway engi-
neers, and the supremely intelligent guy who said, "Hey, why
don't we put a drawbridge right in the middle of this incredibly
busy highway so we can stop millions of cars while one boat
with two people on it goes through." I was angry.

We had talked about this day for a long time. We had prepared ourselves for it. Over long bike rides in the park we talked
of moving across yet another threshold, the empty nest. Yet
when it arrived it was very hard to bear.

The next day I was still in a dark and ugly mood. I couldn't
call Jana. I just knew she'd be in tears. Of course, when she did
call my wife that night, she was happy and bubbly and adjusting quite nicely, thank you. I, on the other hand, was not
adjusting quite nicely.

Jonathan left for his senior year of college on Tuesday. With a
two-thousand-mile drive in front of him he said "So long" as if
he were headed to the 7-Eleven. Again, I stared. And then I
waited for a telephone call that his car had broken down somewhere in Pennsylvania. When the call didn't come I went to bed.

On Wednesday my wife and I went to the beach and had a
picnic. We walked along the dunes, and I was attacked simultane-
ously by fifty mosquitoes. We ran back to the car, and I spent the
rest of the evening scratching.

On Friday my older daughter, Jael, drove upstate for her
sophomore year of college. And we were alone. My wife muttered something to me about opening my own drawbridge so
no one could pass my way, and I knew she was right, but I
chose not to answer.

It is Saturday now, and I am ready to begin another story. And
while the pain is real, the possibilities look inviting as well.
There are so many passages, so many disruptions to the way

things were, so many opportunities to begin new chapters in this life. I have a wise older friend who speaks of the many conversions he has experienced in life. Times of great change when circumstances forced him to think and behave in a new way as he continued on the journey. If life is long we are blessed with many such passages. They can be opportunities for conversion. Or they can be dead ends. And we all decide what we decide.

Throughout this journey, O God of traveling mercies, you inch us onward, cajoling us out of our complacency, moving us ahead one step at a time, more or less. May we put as few obstacles in the way of your prompting as our fears will allow. And may we remove them through your love, embracing the journey and moving on around the bend. AMEN.

7

I Love That Phone

MY SON AND I SAT IN THE UPPER LEVEL, LEFT FIELD, ABOUT TWENTY rows from the top. They were not our regular season seats, but at least we had postseason tickets. The Mets had defeated the Dodgers eleven of twelve games in the regular season but lost in seven games in the league championship series. The game we saw, however, game three, was a stellar win for the fans at Shea, complete with a pine-tar ejection and Keith Hernandez crawling to third base. It was October 1988.

Stuck in a traffic jam on the Grand Central Parkway on the way home, I saw a guy talking on his car phone. I thought, "If I stay in New York one more year, I'm going to have to get one of those."

I stayed in New York one more year. In fact, I'm still here. And I got one of those car phones. It's eleven years later, and until recently I had a smaller, handier version that I wore on my belt when I was traveling. It reminded me of the toy six-shooters I wore at my side when I was a child. The people who sell the phones want you to remember those six-shooters. Now, however, I have a shiny chrome phone I keep in my pocket. I tend to forget about it. I was speaking to a crowd of about a thousand at a convention not long ago when I realized the phone was in my pocket and still on. I tried discreetly putting my hand in my pocket to turn the phone off, but I couldn't find the on-off button. I kept hoping it wouldn't ring during my message.

I travel a great deal, and with the new nationwide one-price programs, the phone is a great convenience—most of the time. There are those days when I'm enjoying a hike in the mountains and the familiar ring starts. It's one of our staff members asking for the telephone number of the marketing firm in Philadelphia.

Then there are those wonderfully dead zones where there is enough of a signal for the phone to ring but not enough of a signal for you to talk with the human being on the other end of the line: "Can you hear me?" "Can you hear me?" "Can you hear me?" "Can you hear me?"

Of course you can hear the other person, but he or she can't hear you. It's your wife telling you the radio station is on the other line, and if she can name the largest city in Vermont within sixty seconds we'll win an all-expense paid trip to Disney World. You shout into the phone "Burlington." And she says, "You've got a bad cell. What was that?" You shout again, "Burlington." But all she can hear is "Sshhkklklksshhshshsh." You look at the display screen, there's just one bar showing on the signal strength meter, and you kiss Disney World good-bye as you can imagine your wife answering "Montpelier?"

Or it's one of your kids calling from her trip back to college. Over the din you hear "And then I sshhkklklksshhshshsh, but everything is okay now." "What?" "I said sshhkklklksshhshshsh, but except for the credit card bill I'll send you, everything's fine."

I was in a business meeting in Louisville not long ago. The Mets had almost squandered a healthy wild card lead in the National League pennant race, but they ended the season tied with the Reds, and a one-game playoff was scheduled in Cincinnati. I dutifully attended my business meeting and the speaker gave us an update one time during the evening: Mets 3, Reds 0. That was the last I heard.

I knew the game must be over. As I was walking into the hotel lobby after the meeting had ended, I glanced at my cell phone.

Three bars jumped up on the signal strength meter, and the phone gave a gentle beep that told me a message was waiting. I called my cell phone voice mail and heard my son's voice: "Hey, Dad, I didn't know if you knew or not, but the Mets won, five to zip. How about that! Love you, Dad."

I love that phone.

May we embrace everything, heavenly God, that brings us closer to those we love. And may we know that everything else is but kindling for the fire. AMEN.

8

Mid-Thoracic to Shoulder Level

THERE IS A SOUND I LIKE TO HEAR. IT'S THE SOUND OF TWO GROWN men hugging and giving each other a slap on the back. The slaps are not gentle. They are hard, at the mid-thoracic to shoulder level, usually three or four in rapid succession. The sound of those back-slaps says to me I am in the presence of a long friendship.

If backslaps like this were done to wives, I'm afraid they would be physically hurt. Not so with men. You might be able to hear the slaps clear across the parking lot, but no one's been hurt. It's just that men have to be hugged hard to feel it. Spouses and children can give a man a gentle hug and mild pat, and his heart is warmed. But from grown men, only a firm hug and a couple of hard backslaps will do. Men are competitors. We stand alone. We want others to think us strong. So the hug must be tight and the slap hard to break through our defenses.

Not just any man can give another man a hug and a backslap. Try to give one before its time, and it'll turn into an awkward handshake. To receive and give hugs, a man must know a man well. He must respect him. The relationship must be mature. It must have weathered a storm or two. The two have seen each other at their best, and they've seen each other at their worst.

The "worst" part is important. All of that, and then it's time for a hug and a hard backslap.

There are only a handful of men with whom I carry out this ritual. I'm close to a lot of guys, but for whatever reason our friendships don't include backslaps. They can't be legislated or planned. They just happen.

My wife and I had dinner with our son the other night in Denver. When it was time to leave, he gave his mom a gentle hug and said good-bye. Then he gave me a very firm hug and two hard slaps on my back, mid-thoracic to shoulder level.

Through offering a touch, God, you brought the apostle Thomas to his knees. Through hugs we feel your love, and power, and presence. May we welcome the warm touch of love. AMEN.

9

Laughter in the Rental Car Bus

I LIKE TO BELIEVE I'M IN CONTROL OF MY LIFE. I CAN SMELL WHEN an airline flight is about to be cancelled, and I'm virtually always the first to book an alternate flight. Often I'm bounding to my new gate before the rest of my fellow travelers realize their travel plans are doomed. My children are aware of my traveling prowess. For the most part they respect it. But they also know a deeper truth.

We were on vacation in southern California, and the entire family was seated in the back of the rental car bus. I watched one of our suitcases wobble precariously each time the van rounded a bend, and I figured I'd better move it to a more secure position. I stood up, and at the exact same moment the driver braked hard. I don't know why he braked hard, but I do know what happened next. I hit the deck and slid all the way to the front of the bus, right to the feet of a couple of businessmen in expensive-looking suits. To this day I don't know why I chose this response, but I looked up at both of them and as casually as possible said, "Hi! How ya doin'?" At which point my entire family exploded into gales of laughter in the back of the bus. Laughter that continued unabated for the better part of three days. Eleven years later, should one of them bring up the story of our trip to California, they all dissolve in laughter.

I couldn't understand what was so funny. The longer they laughed, the more frustrated I became. I could have been hurt. I might have been seriously injured right there before their eyes, sliding down the aisle of the rental car bus. But their first response was not concern for my well-being. Their first response was laughter. It was a good five minutes before my wife could choke out a muffled, "Are you okay?" But even then, before she got out the "okay" she started laughing again. The driver and the businessmen ignored us all.

Now, years later, I think I understand. It's true, I am the kind of man who always likes to appear to be in control. The other airline passengers might end up in long lines and endless delays, but I've already found an alternative. A together guy. But on that day in southern California my family saw graphically portrayed before them what they had known for quite some time—I'm not really in control. None of us are, you know. And the sooner we come to realize it, the sooner we can all enjoy the laughter that comes from being fully human.

God in heaven, God in the rental car bus, thank you for reminding us who is really in charge. Grant us the grace to laugh at ourselves as we realize how little we truly control on this journey of life. AMEN.

10

I Do Miss Those Trees

WE MOVED INTO OUR FIRST AND ONLY HOME IN AUGUST 1982. While we pulled up carpet that revealed beautiful oak floors, painted walls that hadn't been touched in twenty years, and generally spruced up, Jonathan played on the Japanese maple in the backyard. He was five years old. He could just pull himself onto the first branch. From there the world beckoned. With each passing year he climbed higher and higher until the tree could no longer carry his weight. The tree made the transition from jungle gym to stately provider of shade without difficulty, and on many a summer evening we relaxed beneath its branches and the branches of the four other shade trees in the backyard, enjoying the beauty that comes only from northern hardwoods.

The Japanese maple died last year. No obvious signs of disease. It just lost its leaves, then its bark. They came this past Wednesday to cut it down. I also had them take the too-tall evergreen that beauty passed by, the white birch that planted itself way too close to the foundation of the house, and the biggest shade producer of all, the overgrown sugar maple. We get hurricanes every now and then on our curve of the island, and I kept envisioning the sugar maple draped across the bedspread of the master bedroom.

The men who removed the trees were masters of their craft. They kept gauging the wind to be sure wood chips wouldn't fly into any neighbor's yard. Avoiding the power lines was no small feat either. With everything down but the long trunks of the sugar maple and the evergreen I headed down to my study to write their check. With two resounding thuds I heard the trunks fall, and an hour later the backyard was bare. Well, not exactly bare. There are still two oaks by the back fence. But it doesn't look the same.

They put the trunks of the trees in the front yard until they could bring the log loader to cart them away. Every time I walked outside I was drawn to the fresh cuttings at the base of each trunk. All of the trees were at least four years younger than I, but they seemed so much sturdier.

I have always loved trees. The grand old cottonwoods that stand against reason on a dry Arizona cattle ranch. The lodge-pole pines of the high country, so close to God they can't help but reach a little higher and strain a little straighter to touch their Maker. The evergreen of my childhood, with each branch marked by the limits of my climbing courage in those early days of discovery. The dogwoods blossoming white against the gray bank of an early Kentucky spring, just outside the door of the radio station where I got my working start. The gnarled limber pine by Lake Haiyaha that reminds me exquisite beauty is not always symmetrical. The limber pine pictured in our family room. The tree sits atop a rocky outcropping a few hundred feet above Fall River. It has no visible means of sustenance and sup-port. That is, until you carefully follow its roots around granite, over a ledge, and far down through thin air to the rocky soil beneath. Life where all that meets the eye's first glance is rock.

If all of creation is a reflection of the Creator, then I am par-ticularly fond of that part of God reflected in trees. They delight us with oxygen to breathe. Through their shedding of them-selves they help us keep time and encourage the seasons of life.

But back to the trees in my backyard. I hated cutting them down. The children are mad at me. They don't care about rogue storms, but they didn't feel the hard concussion when those trunks fell to the ground. I'm the one who had to worry about us being beneath them. They just loved the shade. It's not the first time I've had to cut down something I love to keep safe something I love more. But then that does seem to be a father's duty. It's the paradoxical nature of love. Still, I do miss those trees. ·

God who goes before us on the journey, the older we become the more lonely we feel. The greater the responsibilities, the fewer there are who understand the challenges we face. May we be ever mindful you risked everything for the sake of those you love. And while there is so much we don't understand, we place our trust in you, the one who risked all. With that love shining the way, we move forward and do what we must. AMEN.

11

Our Children

FROM THE TIME OF THEIR CONCEPTION WE THINK WE ARE their home—they are ours. They come from our love and live and bathe in it through the need-filled days of childhood. We wipe their tears, celebrate their joys, and watch as they create themselves out of the love they feel from our eyes. We see a spark of creativity that comes not from us but is their own and only theirs to know. And we are reminded that they are not really ours at all.

With a prayer we watch as they take flight to test their wings, tethered no more to the limitations we bring. And with our prayer comes the terrible knowing that even in their soaring they are still children, human, vulnerable, prey for the danger that is never far. We draw in a long slow breath, and deep in our prayer we hear the still small voice of our true home saying, "I am with you, and my love is sufficient."

God of our children, the things we love so much are not really ours. You have entrusted them to us, but for a time. Only you can be with them always. May we trust in the truth that your presence is enough. AMEN.

12

Their Work Is Never Done

My wife is exhausted. Our bookkeeper is exhausted. My executive assistant is exhausted. Come to think of it, just about all the mothers in my circle of friends are exhausted.

I know a lot of men who work hard. Some are corporate presidents. Some are senior ministers of rapidly growing churches. Some are entrepreneurs of exciting new ventures. Last week I was with a group of them. They spoke of numbers and bottom lines. Stock prices for the businessmen. Easter Sunday attendance for the pastors. But hard as all of these men work, I don't know a single one who sorts his own socks. Not one changes the sheets on his bed. If you told them they could have a hundred shares of a hot new stock if they could find and install a vacuum cleaner bag within sixty seconds, they'd all groan and sulk. They wouldn't even know where to find the vacuum.

My wife would have those stock certificates in a flash. A third-grade public school teacher, Cathryn brings home two giant canvas bags full of work each and every weekday. She doesn't speak of the net worth of her students or of the numbers of children at her Easter party. She speaks of individual children, naming them with affection and working hard to determine how she might make a difference in that one life. I head to bed after watching Chuck and Sue tell me all the news that sells at 11 p.m. Cathryn is still at the dining room table, her home office, finding yet one more positive way to encourage a third grader with just the right words on a newly graded test. When I'm burying my head in the pillow at 5:30 a.m., trying to drown out the morning call of the mocking bird in the backyard, my wife is already out running with her teacher friend.

Cathryn is also finishing her master's degree, leading a children's choir at church, helping Jael and Jana find apartments for school next year, washing and folding the towels, painting the walls of the basement, and preparing the best lasagna you ever ate. You can't believe it's been fixed by someone whose last name doesn't end in a vowel. And she wonders why she's exhausted?

The bookkeeper at our office is a single mother. She just brought candy into the office for me and Tylenol for herself. She juggles complex accounts at the office while her daughter plays at her feet, peppering Mom with a never-ending stream of the most complicated questions a bright second-grader can muster. In the other room my executive assistant is on the phone checking on her teenage daughter, while in her head she plans dinner for a group of people from church. Then she joins the bookkeeper to take lunch to the disabled retiree whose apartment is in our office complex, covers the travel arrangements for one of our employees, and brings order to my complicated life. And both seem puzzled by their fatigue.

I was reading an article in a demographics magazine that said in families where both the husband and wife work outside the home, the wife does twice as much housework as the husband. The article went to great lengths to show the statistical proof of the findings. That's because men like to dispute it. Men think we're carrying our weight at home. "Hey, I washed the dishes on that Thursday, you know, when you had that thing to go to." To which our wives remind us, "That 'thing' was my study group, and it ended nine months ago."

I do understand the value of men. We do reflect a part of our Creator. But no man gave birth to the Creator when he came to visit this planet. And when he was a child, I've got a feeling I know who came to his rescue when he got sick in the middle of the night.

The mothers in my circle of friends are exhausted because they work harder than the men in their lives. They get less pay and less recognition, and their workday never ends. But they do get the satisfaction of knowing something most men will never understand. The mothers know where the real power lies. It lies with the servants. It always has. There's more power in a pan of lasagna, candy brought into the office, a smiley face on a spelling test, and a phone call to a teenage daughter than in the most successful corporation I know. And thank God it is so.

Male and female you created us, O God. Our differences are not few, and the gaps between us often grow to chasms. Bring us together, God, to understand and appreciate the wholeness that comes when we celebrate one another, all created in your glorious image. And give us respect for the mothers who reflect so beautifully your steadfast love. AMEN.

Just Noticing

1

A Good Man

IT HAD THE MOST COLUMN SPACE OF ANY *NEW YORK TIMES* OBITUARY on Friday, April 17, 1998, five days after Easter.

The *Times* said he graduated from Johnson Bible College, Emory University, and Vanderbilt University. More than likely he came from the same religious fellowship into which I was born. He spent many of his ministry years in Texas, working in a number of different positions, none of which would have caused him to be remembered in the *New York Times*. That is, until November 1963.

Lee Harvey Oswald had assassinated John Fitzgerald Kennedy, the president of the United States. When Oswald was killed less than a week later by Jack Ruby, there was made known the need for someone to conduct the memorial service. Oswald's mother was a Lutheran, so two Lutheran ministers were secured through the local clergy association to conduct the graveside service, the only service planned.

As the one responsible for seeing that the assigned clergy showed, Mr. Louis Saunders drove to the cemetery. He found the pastors balking because of the lack of adequate protection from possible assassins. So Louis Saunders stepped in to do what the *Times* called the shortest memorial service on record. From memory he recited the Twenty-third Psalm and a passage from the Gospels. Then he said a couple of things about Oswald that had been mentioned to him by Oswald's mother. And then it was over.

A good man, doing his job, and thirty-five years later a newspaper eighteen hundred miles away remembered that day when a man brought the compassion of Christ to a broken family in a Texas town. The *Times* remembered him for that one moment of service. But from his actions on that November day in 1963, I've got a feeling Louis Saunders had thousands of such days of service, all largely unnoticed. Except, of course, by the God whose love inspired Louis Saunders to be a man of compassion. But I'm not sure everybody reading the *New York Times* would understand that.

You have told us, God of compassion, there will always be need for light in times of darkness. We tend to think of wars and famine. That is where the light will be needed. Maybe we should think more of neighbors, city hospitals, nursing homes, and troubled families in Texas in their darkest hours. Give us eyes to see, Lord, where your compassion through us should be made known. AMEN.

2

The Toronto Make Believes

WHEN I MOVED TO THE BUFFALO, NEW YORK, AREA IN 1974 I WAS reintroduced to hockey. Not since childhood, when my brother and I would lie awake at night listening across the waters of Lake Erie to broadcasts of the Detroit Red Wings games, had I given more than a nod to the National Hockey League.

But now we were in the outskirts of Buffalo—Sabres country. And the next May they made it all the way to the Stanley Cup before being slashed by the Philadelphia Flyers. When we moved to Buffalo I barely knew a blue line from a restroom line, but I quickly learned the teams to fear and the teams that were not a threat to the Sabres' dominance. One team that was definitely not a threat—the Toronto Maple Leafs. Or, as they were affectionately known on our side of Lake Ontario, the Toronto Make Believes. I always wondered how Canada's largest city could have such a lackluster hockey team. But then there are plenty of things in life I don't understand.

I moved from upstate New York to Long Island about the time the New York Islanders won four straight Stanley Cups. Shortly thereafter they headed on a slide from which they have yet to recover, and I found my interest in the NHL on the wane.

This past week I was in Colorado for the opening of a new church and a few days hiking in Rocky Mountain National Park with my son. We met just east of the foothills where we were to leave Jonathan's car and head into the mountains. When he arrived at the rendezvous point he informed me his tires were out of balance and the car was out of alignment. He'd noticed it before, but on the trip up from Denver it had been pretty bad. I offered to help with repairs, and we headed down Main Street and stopped at the first garage we found. "Yes, we can do alignments and balancing," the owner said. I told him we were headed into the mountains for a couple of days, and I wanted to take advantage of a chance to get my son's car in order.

The owner called the next day with the news that the brakes were bad and that a slow leak had damaged two tires. He noted that he wasn't in the tire business, but he said, "I know how you feel. You want his car to be okay before you head back home." He offered to get the tires for me at another store, plus do the rest of the work needed, and he held the costs down to boot.

We picked up the car the next morning. The owner wasn't there. But on the west wall of the customer area, next to the picture of George Foreman with his arm around the owner, was a picture of the 1977–1978 Toronto Maple Leafs. I asked why the picture was there. The worker said, "Gordon, the owner of the place, the guy you talked to before—he used to play for the Toronto Maple Leafs. That's him on the right on the front row. He was a goalie. He says they used to call them the Toronto Make Believes."

We drove both cars back onto I-25, and I followed my son for a while. When it was time to exit for the Denver airport I pulled up next to him, and he gave me a smile and a big thumbs up. His car drove fine, he was letting me know, and I exited onto Route 7. Happy in the knowing my son was driving a safe car and that a former NHL goalie had been willing to go the extra mile to make it that way.

Maybe Gordon wasn't so hot at stopping pucks from going into nets. But he knows how to make a father's day. And that's not make-believe.

We often have the confidence we know where we will find your kingdom, dear Lord. In the church or the inner-city mission. Serving meals to the homeless or in the search-and-rescue operation. But, Lord, we don't necessarily see you at work in the muffler shop. If we could, our lives would be richer indeed, for if we had eyes to see, we might find your kingdom in lots of surprising places. AMEN.

3

Self-Esteem Way

I TRAVEL A LOT AND HAVE BEEN PRIVILEGED TO BE IN THE "AIN'T Nobody Flies More Than I Do" club for a number of years. One of the perks of membership is that if one is available, I get a first-class seat confirmed seven days in advance of a trip at no additional cost. In other words, most of the time I get to sit up front. And lots of other people who fly a lot are up front too. Including the guy who was with me on a trip from out west a few days ago.

I knew from his suspenders and his conversation with the flight attendants that he was integrally connected with a series of successful books. He had a picture of the books on his suspenders. He promised the flight attendants copies of the books. If I mentioned the books to you, you'd know the name. But of greater interest to me was his briefcase. Well, actually, it was the gold-plated metal nameplate on his briefcase. It had his name, street number and street name, and the town in which he either lives or works. The number and town were common enough. But the name of the street was Self-Esteem Way!

I didn't speak to this gentleman. He seemed to be a friendly and outgoing individual. I believed his promise to send copies of the books to the flight attendants. But I couldn't believe the name of the street—Self-Esteem Way! I have to admit I'd have a pretty tough time either living or working on Self-Esteem Way.

Scott Peck says self-love is healthier than self-esteem. He defines self-esteem as feeling good about oneself at any cost. Pay no attention to the fact you've been a lousy father to your children and a neglectful husband to your wife; you want self-esteem. You want to feel good about yourself, no matter what.

It seems to me there are plenty of times when I shouldn't esteem myself too highly. Plenty of times I shouldn't feel too good about myself. It would be better to see myself realistically, painful as that might be. And to see myself realistically, self-love is necessary. I should love myself. Loving myself includes seeing that sometimes I am a lovely person and sometimes I am not such a lovely person. Self-love is seeing that I'm a project worth working on, no matter how long it takes for me to get it right. Self-love is okay.

But even then, I don't think I'd want to live on Self-Love Way. I like Main Street, or Bayview, or some other innocuous name that won't bring any more embarrassment to me than I already bring to myself. God knows I don't need any help with that.

O Lord, teach us to think no more highly of ourselves than we ought to think highly of ourselves. Keep us ever aware we are made in your image. And keep us ever aware that on occasion we can be a pretty poor reflection of the real thing. AMEN.

4

A Grandfather and a Granddaughter and a War

I WAS FLYING TO WEST PALM BEACH TO CONDUCT AN INTERVIEW for one of our projects. The flight was delayed because of thunderstorms strung across north Florida. We waited patiently at LaGuardia while the storms played out their thundering disruption. Then our MD-80 queued up along with all the other delayed Florida flights and headed for runway 13.

I had noticed a seventy-something gentleman in the US Airways Club a couple of hours before the flight. He looked smartly dressed for a safari, complete with leather backpack, canvas vest, khaki pants, and hiking boots. He also had a pleasant face, an engaging smile, and a bounce in his step that caused me to take notice.

When I am on a plane I usually open the book I'm reading and forego exchanging pleasantries with my seatmate. I may do it because it is the only time I have to read, uninterrupted. But then again I may do it just because I'm not a very outgoing person. Whatever the case, I had already adopted my usual posture on this particular flight when I discovered this same gentleman was my seatmate. He decided to talk, and I decided to listen. I'm glad I did.

He was once a trial attorney in New York and now lives half time in New York and half time in Palm Beach. He's left his law practice to begin a mortgage banking company, which from all appearances has been quite successful. But banking and lawyering were not his major interests on this day. What he wanted to talk about was his granddaughter, American history, and the proud moment when the two came together.

He told me of a trip to Gettysburg with his granddaughter's seventh-grade class. Their history teacher devoted the second semester to the Civil War while preparing the children for a trip to Gettysburg. They were all assigned a rank and a task and taught to prepare for war. As the grandfather explained the trip his respect for his nation was palpable. I would guess he is a second-generation American. Probably he is a World War II veteran, although he didn't say. But seeing his granddaughter learn the price of freedom was a sight he wanted to behold.

When his granddaughter left for Gettysburg he was not far behind. Before the mock battle he poked his head into his granddaughter's tent, much to her chagrin, and wished her well. He knew she was embarrassed by his presence, but he had to speak with her and let her know how lucky she was to be a part of such a moment.

He watched as the troops assembled for battle and charged the enemy lines. One child, assigned to die on the field, sat up from her final resting place and handed him a disposable camera. "Could you take a picture of me dead?" she asked. He obliged, and she thanked him for his assistance. He said he wouldn't have missed the trip for the world.

The attorney turned banker told me his daughter and her husband weren't crazy about the teacher, the course, or the trip. Maybe they thought it was too gory, all this focus on war. But he felt otherwise. Again he spoke of the price of freedom and of the need for children to understand the cost of fighting for something or someone you love.

The flight finally arrived in West Palm Beach, and his family was there, with lots of smiles and hugs. Over the heads of pushy departing passengers I quickly said, "Nice talking with you," and headed off to my meeting. Thinking about a grandfather and freedom and teachers with passion and lots of other good things that made for a fine ride on a stormy day.

There is goodness and passion and love all around, if we would close our book, talk to our neighbor, and have eyes to see.

You exist in relationship, dear God eternal, three in one. We are sustained by relationships. Through them we know love and see our joy complete in the life we share with others. May we celebrate the stories we hear of families who love. And may we love greatly, so others may celebrate with us. AMEN.

5

To Bring Forth the Fruit of a Place

WHEN A LAWYER ASKED JESUS WHAT HE HAD TO DO TO GET INTO heaven, Jesus answered, "Love your neighbor." When the lawyer, pressing his luck, asked who his neighbor might be, Jesus told him it was pretty much anyone with whom he came in contact. The lawyer's response is not recorded.

We had lived in our house on Long Island for a year and had not yet been greeted by one neighbor. To perpetuate what I assumed to be the spirit of the place, I was in the backyard putting a six-foot stockade fence around my property when out of nowhere, there stood my next-door neighbor. She spoke. "You're not going to attach that fence to my fencepost, are you?" She saw my posthole already dug and muttered, "Oh." Then she left without another word. I was sorely tempted to attach my fence to her fencepost. But I gave it a little kick instead. My protest against the state of neighborly affairs as I supposed them to be in New York.

It's now eighteen years later, and I pray to God I'm at least a few years wiser, a few years more accepting, and a few years more neighborly. I've become friendly with those same neighbors. They took my son fishing once. They tell us when our dog gets out of the backyard. We always wave to one another as we enter or leave our homes. I swallowed hard to hold back tears the day she came across the lawn to tell me their youngest son had died suddenly. She said, "A parent never plans for their own child's passing." I wanted to say something comforting, but I stood there and stood there and finally responded, "I'm so sorry."

Jesus had a good bit to say about neighbors. In one story he told of a man who was headed down the mountain from Jerusalem to Jericho, when on a desolate stretch of highway where there was nothing but burned-out cars and stray engine blocks, he was mugged and left for dead. A priest came by, but he was pressed for time. A Levite came by, but he had a budget to balance. And the poor guy by the side of the road was not having a real good day.

But his luck changed when a Samaritan came by. The Samaritan understood something about pain and suffering the priest and Levite did not understand, and he had compassion on the man. First he bandaged his wounds, risking AIDS. Then he put him on his donkey, risking a lawsuit should he fall off. Finally, he paid his medical expenses without government assistance. And Jesus said, "Now that's my idea of a neighbor."

In *Dakota: A Spiritual Geography* Kathleen Norris writes of a saying of the desert monks. "If a man settles in a certain place and does not bring forth the fruit of that place, the place itself will cast him out." I think of that when I gaze out my front window at the houses of all my neighbors and ponder what, with a little neighborliness from me, might be brought to fruition.

Lord, teach me to love my neighbors, one neighbor at a time. Light in me the desire to bring forth the fruit of my place. Teach me to listen and to be there for others, even if it's only to say, "I'm so sorry." AMEN.

6

This Is Communication?

I WAS ON VACATION IN ESTES PARK, COLORADO. MY WIFE AND I had already hiked to the top of Deer Mountain, traveled up Old Ute Trail to the tree line, and negotiated the relatively easy Gem Lake trail. We conversed as we hiked. We talked about all three children and their immanent departures for college, of the adjustments to be made and the bills to be paid. Every now and then when one of us would want to make a point, we'd stop hiking and look each other in the eyes as we spoke. All in all we were having a grand time.

Once I was back to our cabin I figured I'd better check my e-mail. The only motivation I had to read those endless lines of copy was knowing how many more unread messages I would have when I got home if I didn't take care of it while we were on vacation. Since the cabin had no telephone I settled into the utility room at the manager's office, where my six-inch-long computer phone cord left me sitting on the floor. I cranked up the computer, found an access number for my Internet service provider, and dialed in.

There were 8,439 messages waiting for me. Okay, so that's a slight exaggeration. Maybe it was only 34 messages. Camped on the hard floor with my muscles tightening from all those hiking miles, I proceeded to read through each and every e-mail message. By the time I was done I had forgotten I was on vacation.

I like having a computer. I always take my laptop on trips. I particularly enjoy the convenience of word processing. If you have a notion to move a paragraph to the end of a story, with a couple of clicks, it's done. I like word processing, but I do not like e-mail.

So much of communication is visual. "Paul, you're not listening to me." My wife always knows if I'm tuned in. "Yeah, I'm listening." "Then tell me what I just said." "You just said you hope they don't take the children out of your classroom so much this year." "Yeah, but what did I mean by that?" You know how it goes. You gaze into the distance, and your body language tells the true story. To communicate well you need to be looking at the person with whom you are speaking.

It was bad enough when Alexander invented the telephone—a new type of verbal communication had been invented. With no human being to view you had to listen for verbal clues. As we've all discovered, it's nowhere near as easy to hear a stifled yawn as it is to see one. But technology yawns at nothing. It's always moving inexorably forward. And the telephone wasn't enough. We needed computers, the Internet, and e-mail.

A handwritten letter means something. It's time-consuming to write by hand, and it hurts your hand after a while. You have to think about what you want to say and arrange your thoughts carefully. If you've received a handwritten letter you may not be able to see the person who has written you, but you can study his or her handwriting and appreciate the stationery. It may not be a personal visit, but you know someone has given you his or her full attention. Not so with e-mail.

Most of the e-mail messages I receive don't even include a salutation. The person just starts out writing. And forget punctuation or capitalization they aren't necessary just as *unnecesary* as *acurate* spelling. You get the idea. Most of the e-mail messages I receive also don't taper off to a nice "Sincerely, John." They stop cold as soon as the last thought is over. "So let me know if you think we can fit him in this thing or not." And the worst thing about e-mail? Half the messages I get are thoughts that never needed to be expressed. It is okay to have an unexpressed thought.

But enough of e-mail. On to the Internet. In *The Lexus and the Olive Tree* Thomas Friedman suggests the Internet may be the new millennium's answer to the tower of Babel. I think he might be on to something. The tower of Babel took away cultural uniqueness. God restored it when he caused the people to speak in a multitude of languages. With the Internet globalization is again well under-way, and it looks like it's not going to be stopped any time soon.

I thoroughly enjoy the novels of Wendell Berry. His novels speak of people who live in close community, connected to the subtle languages of their ancestors. Anathema to the Internet crowd.

My airline wants to drive me to the Internet with bonus miles and fast reservations. But their Internet provider is pretty pathetic, and I find I can book my reservation in about one-tenth the time with a human being. And the human beings are folks I've gotten to know. One is worried about her son. Another revels in the details of airplanes. They know the sound of my voice, and they affirm me with their genuine "Mr. Williams, how ya doin' this evening?" They speak as though they were expecting me.

The Internet might be here to stay. But God once found a way to deal with human pride and return people to meaningful community when he stopped the tower of Babel with the introduction of more than a few dialects. I don't doubt he has the power to do it again. In the meantime, to all my friends out there who e-mail me, I'll read your e-mail, and I'll probably respond. But I'll be yawning. And by the way, write me a nice handwritten letter sometime, or give me a call. Better yet, stop by for a visit.

May we get on our hands and knees, dear God, to search your face. May we touch the shoulders and wipe the tears of those we love. With smiling eyes may we shake hands with those who sit with us and breathe our air. And may we never be so busy that a warm word, gently spoken by one in our midst, will not reach and touch us to our core. AMEN.

7

"Joy to the World" in the Summertime

WHEN I WAS A CHILD THE SUNDAY EVENING SERVICE AT OUR church had a more semiformal air than the predictable Sunday morning service.

About once every quarter in the early part of the Sunday evening service my father, who was the minister at the church, would ask for favorite hymns. People would call out a hymn from their seats, the pianist would find it in the book, and away we'd go. Most of the songs were predictable. "Amazing Grace" was sung a lot. "How Great Thou Art" was chosen so often my friends and I had memorized its number in the hymnbook—34. Every now and then, even if it was the middle of August, someone would call out the number for "Joy to the World." Everyone knew "Joy to the World" was a Christmas tune, but it seemed to be the Christmas song that belonged to every season. We were always ready to celebrate joy.

Jesus summed it up well in the Gospel of John. "I have told you this so that my joy may be in you and that your joy may be complete" (John 15:11). The pursuit of happiness is a part of the American dream. You go to Disney World for a week to pursue happiness. You buy a new car and hope it will make you happy. We Americans think there's a good chance we can buy happiness.

Joy, by contrast, turns up in the strangest of places. In the midst of the hardest decision you've ever made, when your insides are feeling torn apart, a door cracks open and joy enters the room. In the middle of fighting a life-threatening illness you catch a glimpse of being in the hands of the Almighty, and you are strangely warmed by joy. As you go through the valley of the shadow of death, with the breath of your life being squeezed out of you, joy and laughter arrive unexpectedly.

The pursuit of happiness we Americans think we have down. Joy seems to have a mind of its own. We never quite know when it's going to come. But if we're paying attention, we do know the One who brings it.

God of joy, we have come to know the wonder of surprises. We also know our hearts are most touched when we know the one who has provided them, and we see joy dancing in the eyes of the giver. Thank you for your joyful eyes and deep love. AMEN.

8

It's Swatting Time Again

I AM FAIRLY CONFIDENT THERE IS NOTHING I DO THAT SEEMS flat-out strange to my neighbors.

We once had neighbors who swatted outdoors. At least twice a day we saw them swatting. One year they swatted well into the late fall. I had felt the last itch of a mosquito bite eight weeks earlier. Yet still they swatted. I'm sure there's a place for the proficient swatter, maybe a hot, screenless house along a bayou in late August. But swat outside?

I often wanted to ask, but we seldom talked. I played with my dog in my backyard. They swatted in theirs. I think the neighbor's big dog was the reason for the swatting—I think. It was raining one day. I thought bugs didn't venture out in the rain, even if it meant losing a chance to do what bugs do. Still, beneath umbrellas, they swatted.

The man and his wife were both retired. He swatted mornings. She swatted afternoons. They both came out in the evening. I suppose the dog was grateful. I doubt anyone asked the bugs how they felt.

I wish I had the propensity to better appreciate the swatting of my neighbors, but I tend toward conformity. Rules, regulations, and appropriate behavior. The right outfit for the right occasion. And don't ever do anything that might cause an eyebrow to rise. But I do know people who delight in their uniqueness. They're not captive to what the neighbors might think. If they want to swat outside, they swat outside. They seem at ease with themselves. Fearfully and wonderfully made. No two alike. Along with Walt Whitman they can celebrate themselves and sing themselves.

I need to celebrate myself a little more. Somewhere way down inside I have a hard time believing God's love or anyone's love for me doesn't depend on keeping the rules. Heaven forbid I should march to the beat of a different drummer. Conform. It would be good to find the courage to be uniquely me. To know my inherent value as one made in the image of the Creator. Who knows, I might even step outside with my best flyswatter and take a swat or two.

I am so afraid of judgment, Father. So frightened of standing alone, humiliated. Help me see the outrageous love you have for all of your creation, God. And give me courage to celebrate your image in me. AMEN.

9

The Christmas Bundt Cake

EVERY CHRISTMAS I LOOK FORWARD TO THE COOKIES OUR bookkeeper brings from her mother. They are some of my favorite of the season. This year, for whatever reason, in addition to the cookies we received a bundt cake. As I carried it home on Christmas Eve I realized how light it was. Once home I cut it with a butter knife. Then I ate the best piece of bundt cake I've ever had in my life. It was so good I had to have another. After dinner I had a third, and my wife had a small slice, just to see what all of my expressions of delight were about. I was looking forward to eating more on Christmas day.

With the presents nestled snugly under the Christmas tree, well after midnight my wife and I finally went to bed. I put all the cookies in a Tupperware container and placed the cake on top of the container. Then I pushed both to the back of the counter and headed off to bed.

Christmas morning my wife awoke before I did and went downstairs. She returned to our bedroom and said, "I have some bad news for you. Lilly [our dog] ate the bundt cake. Every last piece of it. She pulled it off the counter and ate it all."

I went downstairs to the kitchen and looked out the back door. Lilly had been banished to the backyard. It was the coldest morning of the year, about 19 degrees. And there was Lilly, huddled against the sliding glass door, shivering. Lilly is a Golden Retriever and has plenty of insulating fur. But I thought, "Sure you're shivering. Every last ounce of circulation you've got is trying to digest an entire bundt cake. There's no blood left to warm your extremities. Tough." I went upstairs.

When I came down again our three children were at the back door with Lilly. The Christmas presents could wait. They had a dog to warm. They took her up to Jana's room, wrapped her in blankets, and fluffed her fur. I looked into the room, and there was the dog in the middle of the bed, with just her head sticking out of the blankets, a doggie smile on her face, and three grown children giving her big hugs.

The dog who ate the Christmas bundt cake was getting all the love they had to give.

Over and over I've eaten the Christmas bundt cake. The bad news is I'll keep eating it as long as I have a mouth to feed. But over and over there is One who loves me, and warms me in his care, and gives me all the love he has to give. And whatever the season, you can build a life on that kind of love.

God of relentless love, I have come to know the painful truth. I will never get it right. Yet your love transcends my disturbing weakness. You draw me into your arms, warm me in your sweet breath, and tell me gently that your love is enough. AMEN.

10

The Obituary Page, of All Places

HIS STORY WAS TOLD IN A NEW YORK TIMES OBITUARY ON Saturday, January 8, 2000. I usually don't get the Times on Saturday, but on this day it was compliments of the Phoenix Airport Marriott Hotel. It was a fine read on a warm January morning.

His name was Robert McG. Thomas Jr. The name was unique, and as the article went on to describe in respectful detail, the man had grown to fit his name. Robert McG. Thomas Jr. died at his summer home in Delaware just a few days into the new year. His wife said the cause was cancer. For the past five years Mr. Thomas had written obituaries full time for the New York Times. According to his employer he had also done stints as a police reporter, a rewrite man, a society news reporter, and a sports writer. His obituary writer wrote that he "developed a knack for illuminating lives that might otherwise have been overlooked or underreported."

What a marvelous thing for which to be remembered. To illuminate lives that might otherwise have been overlooked or underreported. As I read the obituary I realized I had been blessed by a number of Mr. Thomas's stories. I hadn't pulled the loose strings together into a formal thought, but I had found I often lingered on the obituary page of the Times for no discernible reason, reading about people I had never met. I guess at some level I knew there was something special about the obituaries in the Times, but I hadn't paid attention to the wordsmith who brought them to life.

According to his obituary Mr. Thomas saw himself as the sympathetic stranger at the wake listening to the friends and survivors of the deceased, waiting for that memorable tale that defined a life. In 1995 the Times proposed him for a Pulitzer Prize saying, "Every week readers write to the New York Times to say they were moved to tears or laughter by an obituary of someone they hadn't known until that morning's paper." The Times reported one of Mr. Thomas's admirers, a literary essayist, said he got "beyond the facts and the rigid formula of the obit to touch on—of all things to find in the New York Times—a deeper truth."

The article described Mr. Thomas as a "tall man with wavy hair who spoke in a voice soft with traces of his native Tennessee." Describing him as outgoing and gregarious, they said the week before his death he officiated at the annual New Year's Eve party he had been hosting at his home for thirty-two years.

To illuminate lives that might otherwise have been overlooked or underreported. To get beyond the facts to touch on a deeper truth. To preside over a delightful party for thirty-two years. There is something to be said for a person who knows how to celebrate the moment and celebrate a life. We all want a party to attend, and we all want our lives to have meaning. And Robert McG. Thomas Jr. hosted the party and brought the meaning to light, shimmering and dancing on, of all places, the obituary page.

You give us life, Lord, and invite us to infuse it with meaning rich and deep. Fill us with a desire to bring light to the lives of others, and fill us with the joy that comes from a life lived to the fullest. Give us laughter, and peace, and purpose. AMEN.

11

At Least for the Moment

HE IS THE COUSIN OF A FRIEND OF MINE, AND HE NEEDED A RIDE from Brooklyn to Long Island. He is from a town in Poland, Rzeszow. His name is Emil. He spoke no English and I spoke no Polish, and we traveled along in silence on the Belt Parkway. I knew that recently his wife and children had been tragically killed in an automobile accident in Poland. I wanted to find some way to express my sorrow. Somehow he seemed to know.

He took out a worn picture from his wallet and showed me his precious family, and a tear rolled down my cheek, paused at my chin, and dropped onto my jacket. He touched my arm and with a thick accent said, "Thank you. Thank you." At least for the moment the gulf between cultures was bridged, and a grief was observed. And the still small voice of God was heard in the front seat of a Toyota Corolla.

Never allow us to forget, even for a moment, that our hearts can mend, our words can heal, and our tears can convey a oneness you want us to know. AMEN.

The Journey

1

Excited, Terrified, and Called

I WAS FLYING HOME WHEN THE OFF-DUTY PILOT SITTING NEXT TO me said, "What do you do that has you in the air so often?" "Lots of stuff," I replied. "Just trying to make a difference."

In a place deep inside my heart I know God brought me here for his pleasure and for the deep satisfaction that comes from finding and pursuing my purpose. To make a difference in the world. Frederick Buechner says where the world's deep hunger meets your deep gladness is where God calls you. It is important to find one's calling.

Deep inside our hearts is the seed to want to make a difference in the short time we are here. We see work to be done, and we want to do our part to complete it. I have a friend who headed off to the university to be an architect. After the first semester he changed his mind. "Make that a computer programmer," he said. Within a year it was "How about a physician?" With all his changes of heart it took five years to complete a bachelor's degree. But when he finally found his way there was no doubting the call. Even when he worked through the sleepless nights

of his family practice residency he still glowed with the knowing of having found a home.

I don't know how much of my dog's personality is her personality and how much I have projected onto her. But it seems to
me she is fully aware of her purpose—to make the hearts of our
family members beat stronger. To break us from our preoccupied
business to see that a hug and a pat are the foundationally important events. She seems at peace with her calling.

My father was reminiscing about his childhood a couple of
Christmases ago. He said when he was in the eighth grade his
older sister would tell the neighborhood folks, "My kid brother's
gonna be a preacher." Dad says sometimes the people would ask
him to pray. He was glad to oblige. For fifty-four years he's been
preaching. He never looked back.

My children are now finding the joy of turning inside out.
They have been turned outside in since they arrived in this
world. Occasionally they found the joy of serving others, but
most of the time they were busy trying to discover themselves.
Now they realize you don't ever discover yourself until you find
out how you are going to make a difference in the world, who
you are going to serve, and start serving them. Through the wisdom of Jesus they are discovering that those who want to find
themselves must lose themselves.

My heart is profoundly warmed when a person comes to me
after I have preached and says, "I never knew anyone else felt
that way. Maybe I'm pretty normal after all." It confirms my calling. I still remember the time a rather stoic church member spoke
to me after a Sunday worship service. She was a schoolteacher
and a descendent of Abraham Lincoln. I had only recently
started preaching, and I was far behind my contemporaries in
experience. Most had been preaching for four years. I had been
hesitant to preach. Thought I didn't have anything to say.

She came to me at the conclusion of the service and said, "I
think you found your calling." I was both excited and terrified.

Those words stayed with me to this day. Excitement and terror are appropriate responses to catching a glimpse of one's calling. You realize what you might do well. You also realize what might be asked of you.

Jesus knew his calling. And everyone's still talking about it.

Heavenly Father, so often I am full of awe in your presence. Yet so often it feels so awful. To know you want me to join you in co-mission is an honor beyond words, and a terror beyond voice. It is courage I need, dear God, to truly believe the words, your yoke is easy and your burden light. AMEN.

2

On Running Hills, or the Absence of Them

I'VE BEEN RUNNING FOR TWENTY-ONE YEARS. I FIGURE I'VE COVERED about seventeen thousand miles, most of it between three and seven miles at a time, and the majority of it on very flat land. It seems the last Ice Age stopped about halfway across Long Island, New York. It got bored with the trip and stopped, depositing lots of interesting things on the north shore. The dumped stuff turned into hills, while the rest of the island stayed flat as a pancake. That is where I live and run and have my being, in the pancake part.

I run exactly one flat mile from my house through our subdivision of 1950s-built split levels before I get to Heckscher State Park. Then it's another half mile through the woods to the Great South Bay. Another five miles and you still haven't exhausted the hard-packed, sun-baked sand trails of the park. And not a single dip, hill, valley, or incline.

I like the park a lot. I see deer, pheasant, red fox, and migrating birds. I can see across the Great South Bay to the Fire Island Lighthouse and the Atlantic beyond. It's all flat. Sometimes as I leave the park I go out of my way to run over a highway overpass. We call it Heartbreak Hill.

Running over flat land has its rewards. You always know what to expect. No uphills dreaded. No downhill where you can take it easy. Just predictably steady force needed across level terrain.

Life's not like the south shore of Long Island. There are hills and hollows, and every now and then dark mountains with elusive peaks. There are times of great exertion and a precious few long, slow valleys of almost effortless running. It's a long race, and you never know what's around the bend. But if you are paying attention, you know you are never running alone. And that's enough to keep one foot in front of the other.

With me. Ever with me. Above me. Beneath me. To the right of me. To the left of me. Before me. Behind me. Through me, and through me, and through me. This is my prayer, O God. This is my desire. AMEN.

3

The Smoky Hotel

It had not been a good day. After a fitful night of three hours' sleep I wandered through a less than stellar meeting of the board of trustees of one of the organizations with which I work. That was followed by a flight in the center seat of an F-100, which is kind of like trying to sit comfortably in a school locker for two hours. When I picked up my rental car I drove immediately onto the interstate and had traveled exactly twenty-four miles when I first had to use the brakes in any meaningful fashion. And, of course, there were barely any brakes at all. After a few minutes of cautious testing I decided the brakes were adequate to get me where I needed to go, and I drove on.

I would be speaking the next morning for a church where my father had ministered when I was a child. As I continued on the interstate I came to the exit nearest the house in which I lived from ages five to fifteen, and I decided to drive by and take a look at the old home place. I do that every now and then. It's a chance to retrieve memories and make sure the silver maples out front are still growing. The house seems to get smaller each visit. On this particular day, however, the house seemed unusually small. In fact, it wasn't there at all. It was gone, and a small ranch had been erected in its place! How could anyone do that to my house? Now I was annoyed.

I drove on to my hotel, next to 127 other hotels, each standing next to a chain restaurant with the typical Saturday night "We'll buzz you when your table's ready" crowd. I walked into the lobby and said "Reservation for Williams." The young woman behind the counter, seeing my cool mood, responded with professionally calculated reserve. "You're in 1321," she replied. After she efficiently showed me how to get to my building, I turned to leave. I picked up a complimentary copy of the local newspaper and thought about talking with the clerk. I imagined the conversation: "I love the *Beacon Journal*," I would say. "I used to live in town." But I wasn't in the mood for conversation, so I said nothing at all.

When I arrived at my room, it was a smoking room. There were matches and ashtrays and a decided odor. As always, I had reserved a nonsmoking room. With this particular reservation, the hotel even called two days in advance to be sure I was coming. I don't know why, but they did. And they noted that the reservation was for a nonsmoking room.

When I returned to the front desk I rather bluntly said, "That's a smoking room." The young woman replied it was listed as non-smoking, but I assured her there were ashtrays and matches and a distinctly smoky smell in 1321. She passed me along to another clerk who scrolled through the computer screen and announced that all of the nonsmoking rooms were gone. He offered a smoking room that had been ionized, but I simply said, "I'm outta here." And I was. I went to the slightly less comfortable but smoke-free hotel next door and camped out for the night.

Sunday morning came, and I went over my sermon in the shower. Preaching in the shower isn't like singing in the shower. The tile walls don't make it sound any better. The sermon wasn't very good, but I wasn't going to change it one hour before the service. I drove to the church, said my hellos to all those nice folks from my childhood, and stood up to speak.

And there she was, in the second row. The evening clerk from the smoky hotel. Like the younger son in the story of the prodigal son, I came to my senses. The previous evening came flashing back to me—me and my measured abruptness. After the service was over I made a preemptive strike. I asked the young woman, "That guy last night, was he cool and aloof or downright mean?" "Closer to downright mean," she replied. "After you left I turned to the manager, and motioning to the closing door I said, 'Work with me, buddy.' " We both had a good laugh, and we talked for a long time about what it means to be human and the importance of treating other people with dignity, regardless of one's mood.

As I flew on to Atlanta that evening I reflected on the previous twenty-four hours. It had been profoundly embarrassing, but I had to laugh. As long as we are on this old earth, we will be human, and we will have moments like that. And thankfully, the God of mercy and grace understands. Susan, the church-going hotel clerk, knows it, and by the grace of God, I know it. And so it goes.

Merciful. Gracious. Forgiving. They seem more than descriptions, redeeming Creator. They are names for you. They remind us that in your word you did not tell us you love. You told us you are love. And that is enough. AMEN.

4

We Get Letters

I DIRECT A MODEST-SIZED NONPROFIT CORPORATION. WE'RE bigger than a breadbasket but not as big as Rhode Island. Still we're large enough to draw the attention of a lot of folks. Among those folks are a few who don't care for the direction I give to the organization. They write letters and sometimes send them anonymously. If I can tell the letters are anonymously sent I don't open them, let alone read them. I'm not interested in paying a lot of attention to people who don't have the courage to sign their names to a critical letter. But a fair number of those who write with unhappy words do sign their names. Sometimes the letters are thoughtful and kind even though the writer has a bone to pick with me. Sometimes the letters are mean-spirited. I often wonder how I should respond.

I have an acquaintance who sometimes writes on the bottom of a mean-spirited letter, "You may be right." Then he signs his name and returns the letter in a new envelope. Often the letter writers draw grand conclusions based on tiny snippets of information. It is amazing to me how many people understand my motives exactly. It's amazing because often I don't understand my motives exactly. I read one author who in referring to one of those letters that make such grand assumptions said,

"Already condemned I chose not to respond." Not a bad decision, all things considered. Sometimes answering a mean-spirited
letter only validates it. I generally do not want to validate mean-
spirited communication.

When the letters are open and honest, however, it's a different story. To be able to keep growing through life demands we
open ourselves to challenge from the outside. As painful as
many of those letters are they usually contain at least a grain of
truth. I wish I could say I often turn those grains into pearls of
wisdom, but more often than not they sit in my craw agitating
me. But being agitated can be good. It keeps me moving. The
institution of marriage thrives on such tension. Creative tension.
Positive tension. Loving tension. By choosing to spend the rest
of our lives with one other human being we are guaranteeing
ourselves a healthy dose of criticism. If we don't it's probably
not much of a relationship.

In *Threading the Needle,* Lowell "Bud" Paxson tells how he
turned the vision of PAX-TV into a reality in spite of all the
criticism he received. He listed four stages in dealing with criticism. First, anticipate its arrival. Second, assess its accuracy.
Third, make adaptations as necessary. Fourth, move on. Don't
look back. I've known Bud Paxson for quite some time. He is a
man of faith and conviction. He is a true entrepreneur with a
balanced view of criticism. And sure enough, he doesn't look
back. I admire that.

Jesus always seemed to know how to comfort the afflicted and
how to afflict the comfortable. A man turning over tables in a
temple is creating tension. He is being critical. The apostle Paul
wrote a few sharply worded letters as well. I'm sure receiving a
letter from Paul caused a little anxiety. The recipients knew they
were likely to read, "There's good news and there's bad news."

I wish I could say I welcome open and honest critical letters.
But I'd be lying. Whoever wrote, "Sticks and stones will break
my bones, but words will never hurt me," was a tad confused.
Those words hurt. It usually feels like the person is not just

attacking actions of the organization. He or she is attacking me. But still, the voice of God comes from a host of places, and it seems it would be in my best interest to keep on reading. I have no doubt they will keep on writing.

You love us, God, and we are warmed by your love. But we know love does not stand still. It always encourages, hopes, tugs, pulls, and drags us, kicking and screaming most of the way, to become more of what you want us to be. Give us the wisdom, Lord, to know when the voice is yours and when it is the voice of empty deceit. AMEN.

5

The Call

I THOUGHT I HEARD THE CALL OF GOD. A FRIEND SUGGESTED TO me, after a long silence, that maybe God was calling me. I felt the tears begin to trickle and wanted to retreat into my head, but the friend encouraged me to stay in my heart. I did and drove back toward my hotel and called my wife on the cellular phone and told her over a garbled signal I though we were moving. I could barely see the Everett Turnpike through my tears.

But we didn't move. For the most part they seemed to be lovely people, eager to have a senior minister for their healthy church. But when I tried to imagine myself there, most of the thoughts were unsettling. Often I thought about going and dying. Then there's Bonhoeffer—"When God calls a man, he bids him come and die." And there's Jonah, who evidently never did come to grips with the call of God. Is that what it is supposed to feel like to be called of God?

When Moses saw the burning bush and heard the call of God, he had to know, since the bush burned but was not consumed, that he was being called to burn with passion but not be consumed. He responded to the call and saw the back of God but never entered the Promised Land.

I'm well into my forties now, and I know too much. Especially about the many things I don't know. I'm not that sure anymore.

Everywhere I look I see people fearful of truth and determined not to pursue it. Sometimes I live among them. Sometimes I find the courage to take the road less traveled.

I wish God were not so subtle, and I wish God's call was as clear beforehand as it is in hindsight.

Through the collection of life's experiences, Lord, you bring us to the cusp of a life of wisdom. But we must take the final leap to what is seldom clearly known. May we use the discerning hearts you gave to hear your voice calling from the beyond. AMEN.

6

The Other Side of the Mountain

THE FRONT SIDE OF MT. CHAPIN, ON THE NORTHERN END OF Rocky Mountain National Park, is jagged, steep, and foreboding. As you drive through Horseshoe Park and fix your gaze to the north, the routes up Mt. Chapin and both of its kissin' cousins, Mt. Chiquita and Ypsilon Mountain, look formidable to say the least.

For several years I've studied those mountains from the south and east. And for many years I've had no desire to climb them. I'm not into ice axes, pitons, and ropes. I like to hike to a rocky, alpine mountain peak. I don't mind a scramble here or there, and a wide ledge or two to traverse on the way is kind of fun. But on the whole, I like hiking, not climbing. I assumed Mt. Chapin was not hikeable, and I was not interested in a technical climb of a difficult mountain.

But then I discovered Chapin Pass Trailhead. That's right. I discovered it. Two-thirds up the one-way dirt switchbacks known as Fall River Road, the trailhead is the highest in Rocky Mountain National Park. A quick trip from the roadway to Chapin Pass and a right turn through lodgepole pine and krummholz brings you above the tree line to a gorgeous view of

Chapin Creek Meadow and the Never Summer Range beyond. It's only about a mile of hiking along a nice trail at a reasonable grade. After that there is a beautiful valley to the left and a manageable climb up a rock-strewn meadow to a mountain peak on your right. The peak? Mt. Chapin.

That's right. Mt. Chapin, Mt. Chiquita, and Ypsilon Mountain, all difficult climbs from the south and east, are if not quite an alpine stroll at least a reasonable climb when approached from the north.

My son and I attempted Mt. Chapin on a rainy day in September. The monsoon rains had not yet given up their hold on the late summer air, and storms were already brewing. We hiked, nervously glanced at the clouds, and hiked some more. About 300 feet from the top I announced I was going no further. I didn't like the look of a bank of clouds to the west. Jonathan went another 150 feet before a cold rain, a dark cloud, and a news story about fifty-three elk having been killed by a single lightning strike in an alpine meadow drove him back down the mountain beside me. We were mildly disappointed we hadn't reached the summit.

Two weeks later I was in Colorado again. Jonathan drove to Estes Park after class, and we headed up Fall River Road. Elk were bugling, and the long shadows of late summer stretched from west to east. There was not a cloud in the sky. We left the trailhead at four, headed up the path, and then broke off the trail for the summit. After a fair amount of huffing and puffing we were at the rock cairn signaling the 12,454-foot top. We gingerly stepped to the east and looked several thousand feet below, straight down to Horseshoe Park. It was a beautiful hike, and except for a few slips in the snow on the way down, a problem-free day. We were back before sunset. Next summer we plan to reach the other two summits on the route, Mt. Chiquita and Ypsilon Mountain.

I don't find a lesson in every hike. I'm not that ambitious. But on Mt. Chapin I did learn a thing or two about perspective. For all those years I assumed those three mountains were more than I wanted to tackle. Either the hikes were too long or the terrain too treacherous. But that's before I discovered the Chapin Pass Trailhead and the relatively tame back side of the ridge.

The truth is the Chapin Pass Trailhead has been there for a very long time. I've seen pictures of construction workers who built the roadway almost one hundred years ago. I've read of Native American tribes that followed paths over the pass generations ago. The trail itself is well marked and worn. I did not discover the trailhead. In fact, I didn't find the trailhead until the summer of 1999 for one reason: because I didn't ask. I'm confident there were plenty of folks in Estes Park who would have been willing to offer suggestions about seldom-used trails. But I didn't ask.

I tend to behave like a lot of men behave. Drive around a new city for hours but never, ever stop and ask directions. Spend six months trying to put together a bookshelf but never, ever let your handier neighbor help fit Toggle A into Hole C. Self-reliance, we call it. I can find all the trailheads I need, thank you. I prefer the illusion I've discovered them on my own.

I wonder how many vistas I've missed because I refused to invite companions on the journey. How many opportunities have I squandered because "I discovered" meant more to me than "I found a fellow traveler"? For how long could I have enjoyed Mt. Chapin's beauty if only I had said to the friendly clerk at the outfitting store, "Hey, any suggestions about a high country hike in a quiet area of the park?" But no, I had to fully embrace the rugged individualism of the American male.

I think my life would be better served if more often I found the courage to say "Come, walk with me" instead of saying "I've got to discover." Next time I'm in Estes Park, I think I'll strike up a conversation with the clerk at the outfitting store.

I know. I know, Lord. It's about journeying together in community. Whatever it takes, God of growth, keep me moving ever upward, firmly attached to one on the left, and one on the right, and a host of others all around, as we pick and choose, through collective wisdom, the best steps to take us ever higher. AMEN.

7

Barney Fife and the Desire to Be Whole

I OFTEN FEEL LIKE BARNEY FIFE.

There was something powerful yet comforting about Sheriff Andy Taylor. He gave "meek," a misunderstood word, a wonderfully strong face. He seemed gently nourished by small-town life. Aunt Bee's pie and Friday evenings with Helen were enough to keep him steady. That, and the wisdom that comes from knowing one place. He lived close to the earth. I always imagined Andy was real. When the camera wasn't rolling he was still dispensing his wisdom to the mayor, Floyd the barber, and Opie. But as desirable as Andy was I could never get close to him. I could only admire him from afar.

Barney Fife, though, I know only too well. Like Barney, I seem to have an uncanny ability to be an embarrassment to myself. I think we all feel that way. That's why we have a special place in our hearts for Barney.

There was the time the movie company came to town to catch the real Mayberry, and Barney put on the new uniform that made him look like Dudley Do-right. Then the movie director hopped out of his convertible and chastised Barney and the welcoming committee for their excesses. Andy, of course, was standing in the shadows, arms folded across his chest, with the corners of his mouth gently turned up in loving acceptance of all those folk.

I have a difficult time seeing myself the way Andy saw that crowd. I can't fold my arms and warmly accept my own excesses. I stand back in the shadows as Barney Fife, watching the other me, Barney Fife, making a fool of myself before the Hollywood director. And it pains me greatly. There's a vital piece missing from Barney's life. We all know he's not whole. Somewhere back there some water leaked and a short circuit hit the wiring, and everybody knows, most especially Barney.

And most especially me. Sometimes I have to hit the remote control and surf over to CNN Headline News. Barney's embarrassment to himself is too much to bear. Let me hear about White House fundraisers for a while. You know, something that will make me laugh.

We're all broken. Every last one of us. Even Andy's not whole. Yet from the time of our birth that's what we long for—to be whole. We know we were created for more than this. And the journey to wholeness is long and arduous. Andy, Barney, and the folks of Mayberry had company on the journey. That's what we like about *The Andy Griffith Show*. And that's what we hope for in our own lives, fellow travelers on the long and arduous journey to become whole.

Not until we get to the other side, Lord, will we know the full breadth, depth, and love of your reconciliation, your redemption, your sacrifice, and your desire for our lives. May we fully embrace other fellow sojourners, holy Father, so we might journey together toward the wholeness only you provide. AMEN.

8

God Doesn't Talk Much

I WAS FLYING HOME FROM PITTSBURGH WHEN I OVERHEARD the conversation of the two people sitting behind me on the plane. A younger woman and an older man had been talking about the illness of the man's wife. What he understood to be the silence of God through their trials had been very disconcerting to him. The woman offered her thoughts: "God is nothing, if not subtle."

I can drive a long way with my family and never speak a word. I'm not mad at them. I'm happy to be with them. I just don't feel the need to talk. Sometimes I go through the better part of an evening without making a single comment. For me, it's good enough to sit in the family room and listen to the infectious laughter of my son, the rapid teen-speak of my younger daughter, or the fascinating sighs that emanate from her older sister. I might smile or nod a time or two to show my approval, but I'm not driven to speak.

The way I have it figured, it must be that way with God. For over four decades I have been waiting for him to speak to me personally. Oh, I know. He's already spoken plenty, through the Scriptures, through the Spirit. But still, it seems a lot goes unsaid.

I wish God would talk more. When you need some gentle guidance, or worse, a sharp word, it would be nice if he spoke it on the spot. When you see some of the ugliness in the world, it would be helpful if God would say, "Now you're probably wondering about that. Let me explain . . . "

I keep a list of questions to ask God when I get to heaven. The questions aren't unique. I'm sure lots of people have them. Number one. Did you really have to create the possibility of evil for the possibility of love to exist? Number two. What in the world did you have in mind when you created the male/female thing? My list is much longer than that, but I think I'll start there. After I get over the terror of standing before him, I plan to take up a good bit of his time with my unanswered questions.

Then again, maybe I won't. Maybe when I get to heaven, I'll spend the first thousand years or so saying over and over again, "Oh, now I understand."

God of the past and Lord of the future, when Job questioned you, you didn't so much answer as bellow who was he to challenge the one who hung the stars. We understand how little we understand. Help us trust in you, O God. Help us humbly accept that you are God and we are not. AMEN.

9

My Thirtieth Reunion

MY THIRTIETH HIGH SCHOOL REUNION IS SATURDAY. I HAVEN'T decided if I am going.

I didn't go to my tenth reunion. I would have gone, but no one told me about it. I was living 750 miles away. I had been voted "Most Likely to Succeed" during my senior year. But evidently I hadn't succeeded enough to be easily found by those who issued the invitations.

I did get notice of my twentieth reunion, but by the time I learned about it I had committed myself to spend a week in church camp, where I would be encouraging ninety high school young people to develop their spirituality. By the end of the week a little encouragement had taken place, but I missed my reunion.

I really wanted to go to my twenty-fifth reunion. It was time. I wanted to see everyone again and talk about old times. But one of my best friends was getting married that day and asked me to be his best man. So, I went to a wedding instead.

And now the thirtieth reunion. I am away on a study retreat, but my ticket home includes a stop in eastern Kentucky. The thing is, I can't decide if I want to go. Don't get me wrong. I enjoyed high school and dearly loved my classmates. I still enjoy seeing them whenever I am in town, which isn't often. My parents moved away after their retirement ten years ago, and I don't often find reasons to return. I didn't know how much I would miss visiting the place and the people who made it home.

It was a small town, with not much to distinguish it from other small towns. But at an important time in my life it was my anchor. It was home. I liked the laid-back pace, the way everyone knew everyone else, and being called by name when I went into the clothing store. When I return the whole town looks like it's been doing its level best to remain essentially unchanged. Why then don't I want to go back for my reunion?

I think it's about focus. My children are in college. My work is at yet another crossroads. My wife and I are beginning to negotiate a new chapter in our relationship. And I am more interested in the future than I am in the past.

I've learned to make peace with the past. If I am going to linger, I want to linger over thoughts and dreams of tomorrow. What is there that still might be? With a risk taken here and a step of courage there, with a spirit tuned steadfastly toward the right, what might I yet become? If I could go to a reunion where that was the focus I might be more excited about attending. As for Saturday, I'm still undecided.

P.S. I didn't go. I went to Denver and helped my son move into a house he was renting with four other college students. We bought some furniture and stuff, ate a good meal, and talked about God and other things that matter. One of my classmates kindly sent me pictures from the reunion. He included a handwritten description of who was who in each picture. Everyone looked like they were having a grand time. I have no regrets.

God of hope, make my memories linger on thoughts of that which was good, and holy, and life-giving on the twists and turns of my journey. Keep my eyes focused on the wisdom you bring from the collection of stories that have shaped my days. And help me remember, Lord, that the wisdom you bring invites a heart fixed on the return I can yet make in gratitude to you. AMEN.

10

Toward the Outstretched Arms

THE CALL OF THE WILD WAS A GOOD BOOK. I USED TO CALL MY old dog with a single word softly spoken. He always came. I call to my children in the family room, and sometimes they answer. One time my youngest daughter, Jana, came upstairs and said, "What can I do for you, Dad?" I got lightheaded from the strangeness of it all.

I call my friends a lot. The receptionists at their places of business answer. Usually I get to bypass the administrative assistant whose job is to say, "And may I ask why you're calling?" The receptionist puts me straight through. I'm a friend. And then we talk. My friends answer my call.

When I was younger I got excited when I sensed what I labeled the call of God. When I took my first job out of college it felt right. I felt within God's will—confident, challenged, but not overwhelmed—called. But the call of God doesn't seem to come so dramatically any more. Life knocks you around a few times, and what once seemed firmly the call of God now seems a lot more like indigestion.

Now the call of God comes through small events. It accumulates. You're lying on a hillside and the leaves of a silver maple turn in the wind, the cumulus clouds break, and the sun's rays explode onto the summer grass, and you know at that moment you are hearing the call of God. The call says come and take another step forward. You muster the courage and step toward the outstretched arms that always seem just out of reach. And you've answered the call of God.

With aching arms, ever outstretched, weary but never failing, you call us forward, again, again, and yet again. Through fits and starts, Lord, in bits and pieces we come. AMEN.

11

The Really Hard Test

SOMETIMES I MAKE LIFE MORE DIFFICULT THAN IT MEANS TO BE. Don't get me wrong. Life is plenty difficult on its own, but I tend to make it worse than it is. For instance, take the time I passed the test to receive my Federal Communications Commission Third Class Operators License with Broadcast Endorsement. I have no idea why it is lodged in my memory, but I remember the number of the license I received when I passed that test. It was P3-19-25045. For me that test was huge.

My friend's uncle was the majority owner of a commercial radio station in our small eastern Kentucky town. They were looking for capable high school students to become disc jockeys, primarily to work weekend shifts and spell the regular announcers while they were on vacation. As soon as I learned of the opportunity to get paid for talking I was on board. The station had five thousand watts of power on its AM signal and a strong directional FM signal. That meant the entire tri-state area would be able to hear my melodic tones. I was hooked.

There was only one hitch. You had to pass a Federal Communications Commission test to receive a Third Class Operators License. Getting the third-class ticket, as everyone called it, was easy enough. The more difficult test was the necessary Broadcast

Endorsement. That test involved some mathematics, and I never got along particularly well with mathematics.

I knew a few contemporaries who had failed the test. I suppose they might not have studied, and they may not have been particularly bright in the first place. But I was terrified I would soon join their ranks. I studied that booklet like I had never studied before. I wanted to know everything there was to know about the Emergency Broadcast System, appropriate timing for station identification announcements, and all else necessary to pass the test and become a radio announcer. That exam became my Everest.

We had to drive from eastern Kentucky to Charleston, West Virginia, to take the exam at a regional office of the FCC. The night before my big trip I hardly slept. I had visions of transmitter meters flashing past the neurotransmitters in my head. I was a nervous wreck and felt sick to my stomach. The ride to Charleston seemed to never end. By the time we finally arrived at the federal building my stomach was in knots. The examiner handed out the test and told us we could begin. Sweating profusely I began climbing the mountain. I finished the test and returned it to the examiner. Then I went back to my seat and waited for my name to be called. A few minutes later, without emotion the examiner called me to the front, said I had passed, and told me that I would receive my license in a couple of weeks.

I floated all the way home, then went to my afternoon classes at the high school. "Yes," I replied to everyone who inquired. "The test was impossibly hard, but I passed it." For six and one-half years I served as a radio announcer. Throughout that time, I looked up at that license hanging on the wall and remembered the day I passed a very difficult test.

It is now thirty-two years and three months after that momentous occasion. I was at a retreat recently with a friend who was also privileged to get a teenage start in radio. After dinner one evening we compared notes about our respective radio experiences. When I told him how hard I had studied for that Third Class License with Broadcast Endorsement, my friend looked at me as if I had just arrived from some distant planet. "That test was as simple as could be," he replied. "All of the questions were multiple choice. Nobody ever failed that thing. They gave you a little book to study, and that was that."

I protested that the Third Class test itself might have been simple, but the Broadcast Endorsement was indeed pretty difficult. The conversation moved to a different subject, and the retreat continued. By the time I left the next day, I had forgotten about the test. That is, until I flew home the following Thursday. As I sat back in my seat and watched the East Coast stretch out beneath me, I turned the clock back to the fall of 1967 and that FCC exam. I was amazed how well I remembered the day. The size of the room at the federal building. The dark suit of the FCC examiner. The specific classmates who asked how the test had gone, when I returned to high school that afternoon. I even remembered how I felt when I first looked at the test. "Hey, I know these answers," I thought. "I must have gotten one of those rare easier tests." There were a couple of questions I didn't know on the Broadcast Endorsement section, but all in all, not too bad.

The more I thought about it, the more I realized my friend was right. That test was pretty simple. Sure enough, I had friends who had not passed it, but the more I thought about it, the more I realized they had to work pretty hard to fail that thing. It was no big deal.

Why then had my memory rewritten that event? It was simple. It hadn't. In my mind the anticipation of that test was so awful that they could have asked me to sign my name and write the date and that was all, and I still would have thought the test was hard. I made it hard. Really hard. Impossibly hard.

It was not the first time I made this life harder than it is. Nor was it the last. I think Jesus had me in mind when he said, "My yoke is easy and my burden is light" (Matthew 11:30). Some folks have to be kicked in the seat of the pants to take this life seriously. And some of us need to relax a little. We have to be reminded life is here to be enjoyed, and it doesn't always have to be that hard. And we shouldn't worry so much about the test.

Resting in your arms, loving Father, is not easy for those of us who want to get it right, earn our way, reach for the brass ring, and exult in our own accomplishments. Remind us, Lord, that our hearts will never rest until they rest in you. AMEN.

12

The Trek to Long's Peak

IT TOOK ME SEVERAL YEARS TO GET UP THE NERVE TO CLIMB Long's Peak. At 14,255 feet it's the highest point in Rocky Mountain National Park. August and early September comprise the short climbing season for nontechnical climbers. During the rest of the year there's enough ice and snow on the mountain to require crampons and ice axes. The only problem with summer hiking is the thunderstorms. They begin at about one most afternoons, and it's not a good idea to be caught above the tree line when they rumble through.

The trek up Long's Peak is a six-and-a-half-mile hike followed by a one-and-a-half-mile climb. A good friend of mine had climbed it once. He told me about it in great detail. He knows how to spin a tale. It took him three months to get to the top. Vultures were circling overhead. He ate his companions on the trip. He had to dodge orbiting satellites when he finally arrived. You know, that kind of stuff.

I was drawn to Long's Peak and frightened of Long's Peak at the same time, kind of like kindergarten. My son was going to hike all sixteen miles with me. I wanted someone else to go along with the two of us. I find I can say no too easily to my son. He really wanted to get to the top, and he needed a companion more reliable than I.

When Jonathan and I hike together we cover ground quickly. No time to watch the elk grazing. There's a mountain to climb. It is rare for anyone to pass us when we hike. We travel eighteen minutes to the mile when we've built up a head of steam, even on the uphill. Never slower than thirty minutes to the mile.

We needed a fast hiker to join us on the journey, and we found one. Dave flew out from Boston, and we were on the trail at 3 a.m. A veteran above-the-tree-line climber, Dave had his polypropylene shirt, hat, and gloves. He was well prepared for the journey. And how prepared was I? I had jean shorts, a cotton shirt, a cotton sweatshirt, hiking boots, a baseball cap, a flimsy nylon windbreaker, and a watch to see how fast we were climbing. It pains me now to think how ill-prepared I was.

We hit the tree line at about 3:45 a.m. It was windy, and I was cold. We hiked another hour. It was an hour windier, and I was an hour colder. I had never felt so cold in my life. My preparations weren't adequate to the task. I stopped, turned to my friend and my son and said, "Go ahead. This is your dream. It's not mine." To which my son replied, "Yeah, right, Dad. Like you haven't been talking about this since I was twelve." Dave suggested I should sit down behind a boulder to shelter myself from the wind and eat a candy bar from my backpack. I told him to shut up.

That is why I need friends. I understand that courage is not the lack of fear; it's the ability to move ahead in the face of fear. But I don't always want to move ahead in the face of fear. I wanted to go back down the mountain.

But I was with friends. Companions on the journey. People who hear my "shut up" and think, "Who does this guy think he is? Oh well, I'm stuck here with him, so I may as well make the best of it." They don't abandon me. They tolerate me. And they keep me moving forward, more or less.

Jonathan suggested I put my rain poncho on under my windbreaker. I stuffed its long tails into my jean shorts. I looked like a large person with very big hips. And blue lips. And I kept on hiking. We hiked in silence for the next two and a half hours, past the Chasm Lake turnoff, around the base of Mt. Lady Washington, through Granite Pass, and then we switchbacked our way through the Boulder Field. When we finally got to the Boulder Field Campground we stopped for some water. Dave suggested I eat something again. My cold stare let him know I wasn't interested in his suggestions. I still wanted to turn around, but Dave and Jonathan were there. Jonathan had become more than a son when he had responded to my comment about the dream not being mine. He was just another companion on the journey at this point in the process.

We drank some water, ate some breakfast, and scrambled up the last of the boulders to the Keyhole. The sun was just dawning over the crest of Mt. Lady Washington. It was windy and cold, but something changed in me at the Keyhole, and suddenly I was on a quest. I was still afraid, but now I had the courage to move forward in spite of my fear. I was happy and focused and full of energy. We left the Keyhole, headed around the back of the mountain, and up the fifteen-hundred-foot Trough. I was sucking wind in the thin air, and it seemed Dave and Jonathan were supporting me from the rear. You know, keeping the old man moving up. We headed across the Narrows, where with a bit of work you could kill yourself, and I scrambled on, barely aware of the yellow and blue jackets beneath me, trailing further and further behind with each passing step. I wasn't too concerned about Jonathan and Dave. I was on a quest.

I headed up the Homestretch and over the top. There was no more up. It was another minute or so before Dave and Jonathan arrived. Dave didn't look so good. He was having altitude problems. Seems it's not a good idea to leave sea level at Boston and be at 14,255 feet in Colorado less than twenty-four hours later. Jonathan didn't look so hot either. He had a cold, and it had gotten the best of him. An antihistamine at 14,255 feet does strange things to your stamina.

Yes, the two of them had struggled the last mile and a half while I climbed ahead higher than a kite, on a quest, alone. They trudged along pushed only by their determination, receiving not one lick of encouragement from me. I was off in the distance humming my solitary tune.

It took us four and a half hours to get to the top. I figure for about fifteen minutes of that trip I was a sane and rational person. The rest of the time I was profoundly unaware of my need for my companions on the journey.

After a Snickers bar and some water we headed back down. We descended the Homestretch on the seats of our pants, gingerly stepped across the Narrows, and worked our way back down the Trough. By the time we got to the Keyhole there were blisters enough to go around. We rested for a while on the sunny side of the Keyhole and then trudged off through the Boulder Field. Dave was still suffering oxygen deprivation. As we worked our way over the switchbacks below the Boulder Field he had to be caught up by the two of us a time or two. Jonathan and I walked on either side of Dave and gave him a nudge in the right direction when needed.

After miles of switchbacks we were back below ten thousand feet. Dave's altitude problems were gone, and I was back in my right mind, such as it is. Jonathan's Achilles tendon was giving him some trouble, but he was otherwise in fine spirits. I had already discovered on the way up where my Achilles heel was. As we headed down the lower part of the mountain we talked, and the conversation was good. We traded stories about prayer, families, the Mets, the peaks of New England, and friendship. We feasted at an Italian restaurant that night back in Estes Park. And when we walked out of the restaurant and turned toward Long's Peak, I said, "The three of us. We climbed that mountain."

We climbed the mountain again two years later. On the second trip Dave and Jonathan got to the top before me. I'd like to say I had more determination than on the first trip, but the truth is I would have quit again, if it hadn't been for the two of them.

I often think I can make it on my own in this life. I don't know where I got that idea, and when I'm in my right mind, I wonder who I'm kidding. I read recently that some quantum physicists think the only reality is relationships. I don't know much about quantum physics, but I do know how I got to the top of the mountain.

We want to climb, God. We want to soar, to stand at the top where there is no more up. We want to have it all, and we want to do it all by ourselves. Of course, dear Lord, you did not design us that way. Even you exist in relationship, Father, Son, and Spirit. Thank you for creating us with a need for friends on the journey, for their graciousness, their mercy, their companionship, and their love. AMEN.

13

pilgrim62

THE E-MAIL ADDRESSES PEOPLE CHOOSE ARE A SOURCE OF INTRIGUE to me. I have one friend whose e-mail address is his last name followed by the symbol @, and his particular well-known Internet service provider, followed by .com. This friend was one of the first to get an e-mail address, and he has an unusual last name. He's one of the lucky ones. Not so for the rest of us.

According to the folks at my Internet provider I am about the twelve millionth Paul Williams on line. When they suggested e-mail addresses to me they included such thoughtful recommendations as "paulwilli347" and "pwill2594." Thanks for the creativity.

I have one friend who has an interesting e-mail address. It is pilgrim62. I asked him about it once as we drove to a human rights committee meeting in West Virginia, where we both serve as board members of a nonprofit corporation. He told me he chose the name pilgrim, but his Internet provider informed him he was not the first person to have that idea. They suggested pilgrim62. I was encouraged by their suggestion. I'm not sure exactly how the selection of addresses occurs, but it seemed to me that at least sixty-one other people in the state of West Virginia had wanted "pilgrim" as an e-mail address. I thought that was good news. But then I have an affinity for pilgrims.

Life is a spiritual journey. It is a pilgrimage. I am a pilgrim. Ask the typical American grade school child what a pilgrim is and she will tell you about the Pilgrims, that early-seventeenth-century group of British Protestants who believed so much in their spiritual journey that they headed across a treacherous ocean in rickety old ships to continue their pilgrimage. When I asked one of my daughters why the Pilgrims came to America she responded that they wanted religious freedom. "Freedom to do what?" I asked. "Freedom to pursue happiness, I guess," was her reply. I doubt it is an atypical reply. After all, it's in our Declaration of Independence. Surely anyone coming to America wants to pursue happiness.

But the Pilgrims seemed to understand it wasn't about happiness. That's a good thing because in the books I've read about their experience in the New World, happiness wasn't abundant around Plymouth Rock. The reason they came to the coast of Massachusetts was to pursue their pilgrimage, their spiritual journey. It wasn't about covering miles from point A to point B. It wasn't about a once-in-a-lifetime trek to their Mecca, the coast of New England. They came because they saw all of life as a pilgrimage, a spiritual journey. The geography was not relevant. They wanted a place where they could continue their collective journey.

pilgrim62 doesn't leave West Virginia much. He's not a world traveler or a corporate vice president. He doesn't shop at Nordstrom's or drive a large sport utility vehicle. He seems to be happy, but he didn't choose happy62 as an e-mail address. He knows first and foremost he's a pilgrim, on a never-ending spiritual journey with marvelous twists and turns, hills and valleys, right there in the middle of his head and his heart in West Virginia.

My friend delivers mail on a rural route. He drives a usually dirty Subaru with the steering column on the right hand side so it's easier to deliver the mail to the rural mailboxes. On Sundays he preaches at a country church that has been around for generations. When we attend the human rights committee meetings he treats every individual as if he or she is the ambassador of an important foreign nation. Every person deserves his or her dignity, and pilgrim62 is there to be sure they receive it. He listens intently to every word spoken by every single person. For those who have developmental disabilities and have a difficult time speaking, he leans in close and gives voice to mouthed words. Many of the others in attendance at the meetings have a similar patience, understanding, and love. I've never asked, but I wouldn't be surprised if pilgrim58 and pilgrim14 were among them.

I'm the guy in the Nordstrom jacket and the cell phone, nervously looking at my watch wondering when the meeting will be over. I've got a plane to catch. My e-mail address is the name of the corporation I lead, followed by my first name. That ought to tell you something.

I am very glad pilgrim62 is in my life. Every time I am with him I slow down a little, breathe a little easier, and find him leaning in close to give voice to my mouthed words. We talk about the ongoing pilgrimage we share and of the Spirit who gives voice to the unmouthed words from both of our hearts. And knowing him as I do, it warms my soul to think there might be at least another sixty-one computer-owning, Internet-wired people in West Virginia like him.

Through ears turned to whispering lips you make yourself known. Through simple lives lived with joy and harmony you make yourself known. Through fellow travelers on the journey you make yourself known. Thank you, God of all pilgrims, for calling us on the journey and for walking with us every step of the way. AMEN.